D0330354

Homeless in Paradise:
Communicating with the Bohemian
Venice Beach, CA Sub-culture

William G. O'Connell, M.A.

Editor
Jane A. Lackner

Contributing Editor
Dominick J. Castaldo

© Copyright 2008, William G. O'Connell

To arrange for William O'Connell to speak at your high school, college,
corporate event, or as a motivational guest speaker email

To contact the author or his film crew:
americanflag63@yahoo.com

Surferboy Networks©
Webpage: www.williamoconnell.net

All Rights Reserved.

No part of this book may be reproduced, stored in a
retrieval system, or transmitted by any means,
electronic, mechanical, photocopying, recording,
or otherwise, without written permission
from the author.

ISBN: 978-0-557-03501-4
Distribution Publisher: Lulu Publishing
Lulu.com

SPECIAL NOTE: BY PURCHASING THIS BOOK, PLEASE
KNOW THAT IN GOOD FAITH, A PORTION OF THE PROCEEDS
FROM THE SALE OF THIS BOOK WILL BE DONATED TO THE
LEUKEMIA & LYMPHOMA SOCIETY, LONG ISLAND CHAPTER
FOR CHILDHOOD CANCER RESEARCH AND EDUCATION
MATERIALS FOR CHILDREN AT THE LOCAL HOMELESS
SHELTER.

A NOTE FROM COLIN: My Dad said that this book is suitable for audi-
ences over 18 years of age only.

# Dedication

This book is dedicated to my son Colin J. O'Connell whose fight for life at the age of seven months from a rare form of Leukemia changed my life as a parent. Colin is my hero!

Often times we go through life not knowing what to expect. Never, did I think I would meet such unbelievable people when we had to hold a Bone Marrow-Blood Donation Drive in East Islip, NY in order to find a donor match for Colin who was clinging to life. Thank you to the dedicated people in our community, around the country, and especially the doctors and nurses who serve Schneider Children's Hospital in New Hyde Park, New York. If not for Chris Simmons of Davidson, North Carolina, Colin would not be here. Thank you Chris, Angie, Peter, and Anna for giving my son the precious gift of life.

One in two people die from Acute Myelogenous Leukemia in the United States. Please take the opportunity to donate a dollar to Colin's cause so that we can give children a fighting chance to win the battle against childhood cancer.

Go to our Leukemia and Lymphoma Society Website at:

http://www.active.com/donate/dollarforcolin

Acknowledgements:

First and foremost, I would like to thank Jane A. Lackner for all of her contributions to this book. Jane played such a crucial role in the success of this book as she placed herself in harm's way many times. Jane also played a pivotal role in balancing some of the most difficult interviews obtained. I want to acknowledge her son Daniel, and respectfully, the memory of Billy Lackner, Jr., whose spiritual butterflies make the world a better place.

Next, Dominick J. Castaldo, my best friend, assisted me, and guided me. I will be forever grateful for his gift of friendship along with his wife Iris. Also, thanks to my other best friends, Raymond Cooper, Kevin Casey, and Patty Hamill and family.

I thank all of my students at Nassau and Suffolk Community College who supported me from the beginning to the end of the book, constantly showing interest, and pushing me to complete it.

In memory: Rhonda Gaboff, Child Life Specialist at Schneider Children's Hospital, killed by a Drunk Driver. The memory of my father Daniel J. O'Connell lives on forever.

Special thanks to: Leukemia & Lymphoma Society, Long Island Chapter Executive Director, Tammy Philie, Logan Sappell, Dina Matera, and Glenn Schifano, Music Therapist.

My Family: My mother, Sylvia, her husband, Joseph Romero, Debra, Paul, and Paul Michael Bucking, Robert O'Connell, Paul, Ryan, and Anna O'Connell, Jennifer, Brian, and Lucas Knoerzer, Maureen, Richard, Lauren, and Emily Lavacca, Gloria, Amparo Crespo, Wilfredo Sosa and family, and the Ewald family: Michael, Mary, and Michael Jr.

Finally, I would like to thank the entire Language and Communication Arts Department at SCCC Grant Campus, especially Dr. Sandra Susman-Palmer, M. Bernadette Garcia, Dr. Yvon Joseph, Dr. Daniel Awodiya, Alyssa Kauffman, and Campus Dean, Dr. Shaun McKay who constantly asked me about my book. Also, my on location film Crew: Legit Productions, David H. Dickinson and crew. Web Designer: Chris Sforza.

Don't be fooled by the publisher. I had four official contracts offered for this book in writing and in the end, I decided to use Lulu, one of the world's best because they were the best fit for me. When choosing a headache free distributor for your book consider this company—they are awesome!

 Forward

By Tammy Philie,

Executive Director of The Leukemia & Lymphoma Society's Long Island Chapter

In Homeless in Paradise, Communicating with the Bohemian Venice Beach Subculture, author Bill O'Connell explores one of modern day American Society's epidemics, homelessness. We are taken to Venice Beach, CA, a community that in and of itself illustrates the co-existence of diverse economic spheres living in "harmony". We are introduced to many individuals whose stories most of us cannot relate to, but we know exist, and that they are nonetheless no different than someone else who is homeless in Any City, USA. We are asked to get to know them, and by doing so, we can begin to scratch the surface and understand homelessness in America.

By definition, epidemic means a temporary prevalence of disease or a rapid spread or increase in the occurrence of something. Throughout many decades, American Society has learned to streamline this definition to apply mostly to disease and illness, something that can happen to anyone regardless of their actions, and something that can be "cured" with enough funding for the best research and the discovery of the right antidote. When used outside of the physical disease category, we can find it describing hunger and poverty in Third World Nations because we are told of corruptive governments, natural disasters, and/or simple lack within their environments that affect the ability of people to support their own existence. Once again, something that is considered out of the people's control.

Most people don't consider homelessness or even poverty in America an epidemic. We can't and won't because by design because capitalism teaches us that we all have the "freedom" to strive to be anything we want, regardless of where we came from or where we are now. We believe this, we built a country on it, and therefore homelessness does not "fit" neatly into our model or design. It goes against our cultural understanding in that we cannot comprehend why there are people who have nothing, no where to live, when we live in a Society where you can have anything? We conclude that "these people" must have chosen that existence. Yet, as Bill O'Connell demonstrates, it does exist for a variety of reasons described in this book, and we are forced to ask ourselves many questions along the way.

As the Executive Director of The Leukemia & Lymphoma Society's Long Island Chapter, the organization that is responsible for the progress made in the therapies that saved Bill's son Colin's life at 2-years of age, I can say it is *because* of our passionate organizational commitment and focus to cure blood cancers and improve quality of life for patients and their families, that we have made such great strides in our treatments and we will find a cure. We do educate people as to why it is important, and we know that by doing so, they will do something about it and that they want to. Consequentially, the creation of this vehicle of possibility aimed toward manifestation of our goals ultimately provides hope for all cancer patients, and thus the vision of a better tomorrow can exist. We would not be able to do so if people ignore the reality of it's existence or even it's progress. My task is an easier sell though, because of the way we think about disease, that it can happen to anyone regardless of their actions, and that it can happen to us.

Prior to reading Homeless in Paradise, I can't say that I really understood anything about homelessness. Like most, I could not relate to it. This despite the fact that I have committed my life to find cures for blood cancer having never been personally affected. I now ask, why can't we think the same about homelessness as we do about disease? Why do we see it differently? We as a Society need to examine what is really happening in the world around us, and our perceptions in the face of that reality. We need to question, as Bill does and asks us to do. By doing so, we can identify the need and work toward making progress in the area of homelessness. This will create a better reality for ourselves, our children, and for future generations. We MUST ask these questions because by doing so, we are inviting the solutions. By acknowledging that diseases, poverty, and homelessness, are all areas that need to be understood and eventually eradicated, we can pave the way to turn obstacles into opportunities that will result in the advancement of civilization. We will become an even better form of Democracy, society as a whole, and a model for the world. Isn't that our purpose and the purpose for humanity?

Table of Contents

Part 1

Chapter 1

Welcome to Venice Beach

Photo: William G. O'Connell

A view from the balcony of the author's apartment on July 4th weekend as hundreds of thousands visit Venice Beach.

It was six thirty in the morning and I was stretching my legs before going for my three-mile run to peaceful Santa Monica and back. As I looked up from stretching, a man walked from the beach to the Venice Beach Ocean Front Walk in a pair of blue jeans, an open white shirt exposing his tan, toned body, with a big smile on his face, bright white teeth, a goatee, short brown hair, and no shoes. Walking over to the

3

water fountain, he sipped the water, dropped his bedding mattress, and glanced at me.

After observing him for years, I made up a nickname for him. I call him Papillon (pronounced PAP-ee-yon). The guy reminded me of the character Louis Dega, played by Dustin Hoffman, with Steve McQueen from the 1973 movie *Papillon,* a movie about a man who befriends a fellow criminal on a dreadful prison island and the two plot an escape. I said hello, but did not get the sense that he was acknowledging my presence. Suddenly, he then stood straight up at attention, closed his eyes slowly while moving his head from left to right lowering his chin, and in a very expressive English accent, with eyes flashing, he declared, "You are to brush your hair properly with a crease in your scalp, scrub, and I bloody mean scrub your teeth, Piggy, eliminate the fleas and odor from your body, and wipe that grin from your smiling ugly face before I slap it off to Tunisia." Welcome to Venice Beach, California, the Greatest Show on Earth, where befriending the homeless is an adventure beyond adventures and one of the most interesting rides of my life.

According to Merriam-Webster's Collegiate Dictionary, the definition of homeless is not having a home or permanent place of residence. This definition fails to convey the gravity of the word. How serious of a problem is homelessness? This question may be easy to answer for those who advocate on behalf of homeless individuals and families—but so long as any one person is homeless, the problem is too great.

I wrote this book about homelessness because I have an incredible story to tell. Like so many people in America, I don't believe that this crisis would have made an impact in my life had I not met so many homeless people. I used to believe that homeless people are homeless because, after all, it is their choice. My entire perception of this unpopular segment of American society changed on a brisk April day on Venice Beach, California when I was exposed to a homeless Vietnam veteran named Pruitt. As a result, I realized that homeless or not, we all have a story. I started to care about the homeless faces I met, and now, I will never again assume things about the homeless. I spent more than a thousand hours with homeless people, more than twenty weeks of back-and-forth living from Los Angeles to New York, and never did I think I would take back the incredible life altering memories that I have built learning how to survive through the lives of homeless complete strangers, seeing Venice Beach and life from a completely different perspective.

On a larger scale, trying to find the best way to understand this social problem, I thought the best way to approach it was to meet the problem face to face with people I knew had deep-rooted problems, so that I could begin to see the world through their eyes. It was a unique and life-altering experience because I found I could now empathize with the homeless by learning their stories with some of them bringing out the very best in me personally. They made me question life's purpose.

You may be asking yourself, "Who cares about these people?" Readers will be able to answer some questions about the homeless they may see in their communities as to why people become homeless. They will discover that many of the homeless are mothers, fathers, sisters, brothers, sons, and daughters who are down and out or who stepped away from or got caught up in the pressures of everyday life, drug abuse and addiction, alcoholism, domestic violence, or just absolute tragedy. Everyone on the planet has a different way of coping with problems, but when the problems seem bigger than life and there is nowhere to turn, some homeless make decisions that sometimes cost them their life.

The scope and aim of this book is to go beyond answering these assumptions about what is presumed to be a bunch of homeless people who made the choice to live this lifestyle. I want readers to live the experience through the eyes of the homeless. I want you to feel their pain, and, most importantly, to understand their deepest thoughts and why it benefits us to be compassionate enough to care.

August 2007: The Silent Battle

"Make your life count." This motto is what my mentor and college journalism professor, Karl Grossman, taught me when I was a college student. Over the years, I have done my best to live by those words. I have always loved learning and helping people because it makes me feel so good about myself at the end of the day. Karl inspired me to make a difference! It is a difference that I am determined to make.

As I tell my students each semester, every second, minute, hour, day, week, month, and year in life counts, beginning with the morning I sat at the outdoor café on a beautiful early August day enjoying breakfast in Venice Beach, California with my loving partner, Jane. A man drew near us slowly in his wheelchair, holding an ageless hat that read 'Vietnam Veteran,' and he had a fatigued look to him. I couldn't help but cringe as I realized that the nice bacon and egg omelet I was eating was no longer appealing. I listened to the laughs and saw the smiles of the patrons sitting in the outside café enjoying their breakfast, but then I focused on the veteran. Everything about the veteran looked worn. He had on an ancient military jacket and dirty ripped jeans, and his face was weathered and tanned from the elements. Looking into the veteran's eyes, I could only guess at his pain, the pain of so many people in his condition who have no soft bed to sleep in and always wonder where their next meal will come from. The man and I never spoke, nor did we have to. Sometimes spoken words are not necessary to describe a person's pain. That instant our eyes met, I looked back at the world and the homeless from a different vantage point as I opened my eyes to the reality of their lives and the people who occupy our physical world. This was a homeless man who served his country. It was obvious that the man was disabled and not playing a scam on the public, yet still he was homeless. A few tears rolled down my face. To make life easier for the veteran, I gave him a few dollars, which was all I had, and watched him buy some coffee and a roll. I couldn't imagine my own father being in this predicament. As the veteran rolled away in his wheelchair to buy his meal, he pushed his way to the corner of a convenience store and just sat, staring and thinking, seemingly grateful for the food he consumed.

There are all kinds of horror stories out there about our homeless veterans. Less than a year after serving with the 3rd Infantry Division in Iraq, twenty-five year old Herold Noel found himself unemployed, homeless, and unable to provide for his wife and four children. The veteran suffers from Post-Traumatic Stress Disorder living out of his car in Brooklyn. Instead of being greeted by a support system for veterans, Herold met resistance from the Housing Authority, the VA, and New York's city shelter for families, filling out form after form and added to waiting list after waiting list. The fact that there is a waiting list only illuminates the problem (Guerilla News Network, Jan 2005).

Our vets deserve better. VA hospitals are not equipped to handle the demands of these war destroyed vets. The notorious Walter Reed Army Center serves as a reminder of how the VA fails veterans. The bureaucrats keep telling us that veterans have many benefits. Already, the Veterans Affairs Department has identified "1,500 homeless veterans from the current war and says 400 of them have participated in its programs specifically targeting homelessness" (Guerilla News Network, 2008). Then why is one of every four homeless people in this country a veteran?

Why should we as a people, as a nation, leave our brothers and sisters on the streets to fend for themselves?

Surely, our government can create a "pilot" plan to gather the hundreds of thousands of homeless veterans to get them the help they need and not some wishy-washy plan which leaves many vets in a state of disarray. Even a basic food stamp plan would help these people. Many homeless don't know how to go about getting food stamps. I asked many and one replied, "The government will not help me because I am a drug user."

This was the beginning of my endless journey.

Chapter 2

Venice: A Colorful Conscious Evolution

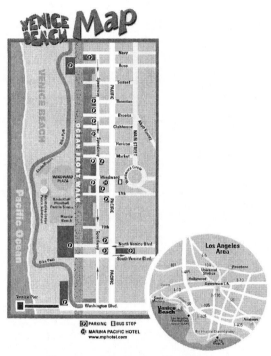

Courtesy: Marina Pacific Hotel

I chose Venice Beach because of the worldwide appeal it has. Since the time I was a child, I was fascinated with the California scene, the hippie culture, surf life, climate, and its colorful characters. I also felt it is the one place of all the places I have traveled to where I felt a true sense of freedom and commonality amongst Americans. Living in Venice opened my eyes to what I am missing in New York, especially the alluring beach community.

Venice Beach, California is a desired destination for travelers from all over the world. It is unlike any place on Earth, well known for its artists, street performers, and funky atmosphere. It is a virtual carnival running year round with free admission. I hail from the beaches of Fire Island, an idyllic beach community on Long Island, New York.

The first thing I noticed when arriving in Venice Beach is the different modes of transportation. In Venice, no cars are allowed on the walk. I have never seen so many men, women, and children using skateboards, roller blades, and bicycles to get around. Perhaps what makes Venice Beach such an interesting place are the lively carefree characters that inhabit this beachfront community.

I would describe the Ocean Front Walk on Venice Beach as a compact "Main Street" surrounded by beach bungalows and back alleyways that lead to the surf and sand and back to Main Street, which doesn't quite have the hustle and bustle of traffic that nearby downtown Los Angeles has. Within a short distance from Venice are Malibu, Beverly Hills, Hollywood, and Marina del Rey.

Venice is a haven for business people, beachcombers, drumcircles, starving artists, aspiring musicians, card readers, healers, surfers, bikini skaters, belly dancers, bikers, drug and alcohol users, street performers, conformists, non-conformists, and, finally, countless dog walkers. Many Venice Beach store owners even allow dogs into their shops, and as patrons sit to eat at any of the outdoor cafés along the walk, dogs are welcome in dog town.

In laying out the Venice terrain, I will be talking throughout the book about a few locations. First is Rose Avenue, (See Map Page 10), located just a block from the beach. Then there is the Ocean Front Walk, which sits directly on the beach where Dudley, Speedway, Brooks, and Henry's Market (owned by my friend Shyla) do business, which is just over one mile to the south of Santa Monica and one mile to the north of Washington Avenue in the opposite direction which is within walking distance to Marina del Rey. Many of the best restaurants in Venice are located on Washington, which is a hot spot for most tourists. The central location of where the most activity occurs for us is in this area.

The Santa Monica Mountains and Malibu Canyon are a beautiful sight from Venice, and they become clearly visible as the hot California morning sun burns the fog in the sky away.

As I sit and wonder about the colorful history of Venice Beach, it is hard not to reflect on who had the vision to build this place. One thing Venice is not is ostentatious. It is a community, which invites tourism because of its flair and intercultural diversity. "As early as the 1890s, Southern Californians were showing an intense relationship to the stunning shoreline that fronted their mountain-and-desert-guarded enclave." You know the saying "we can't appreciate what we don't have"? Venice Beach has!

As far back as the late 1800s, before the turn of the century, Middle-class families would spend an entire month on the beach living in tents. Their time was spent basking in the sun and playing in the surf, while experiencing adventure; but for the homeless, the beach sand, the cement walk, and the ten-foot-deep space that separates one building from the next is home to many.

In a magazine article written by Arthur C. Verge, California History, titled "George Freeth: King of the Surfers and California's Forgotten Hero," Verge writes, "Los Angeles in 1907 was undergoing a large growth spurt both in population and business formation. Venice and Redondo Beach were centerpieces of real-estate development along the region's stunning coastline. Venice Beach today, still looks old and many of the old buildings still stand, but it hasn't stopped tourists from visiting the beach" (Verge, 2001).

Venice Beach is no stranger to publicity either. According to the Los Angeles Conservancy, the "Venice of America" known as Venice Beach today "was founded by Abbott Kinney in 1900, and opened in 1905. Kinney turned his attention to an uninhabited mile-and-a half stretch of oceanfront property." Kinney was one of four partners in a company called "The Oceanfront Improvement Company" devoted, not surprisingly, to improving the oceanfront for people (Los Angeles Conservancy).

In those days, people would sometimes use a coin toss as an honor system to resolve a disagreement. In this case, "Kinney won the toss, and his share of the property he had with his partners after the company dissolved, and then he came up with a plan. Its holdings were subdivided with Kinney choosing the undeveloped portion of the property in the coin toss." Voila, Venice Beach is born.

The area of the Venice canals gave Kinney the vision to replicate the Venice of Italy, and "he set about building a community that he hoped would foster a cultural renaissance in America." Kinney also envisioned a resort town that "was culturally reminiscent of its Italian namesake, complete with canals, gondolas, amusement piers, hotels and Venetian-styled structures," many of which still stand today.

But by December 1905, "Kinney realized that his dream of creating a Mecca had failed." Being the perceptive businessperson that he was, "he turned his attention to accommodating the wishes of the public" (Los Angeles Conservancy, 2008). That wish made Venice into a colorful subculture mixed with every walk of life one can imagine.

More than one hundred years later, not only has Venice Beach survived, but also it has soared in popularity. Kinney's vision makes many residents and tourists from around the world who visit Venice happy. People enjoy spending quality time at the canal watching the ducks, herons, and other birds living at the bird sanctuary off Washington Avenue. This is a nice section of the canal, and the street has many restaurants and shops.

Two hundred feet from the canal is the Inn at Venice where we stayed for a few nights. Have breakfast in the morning and you will discover an entertaining place!

By the way, do not feed the ducks; it is illegal!

Fast forward from Kinney's inspiration to the 1960s and we "break on through to the other side," and learn that Venice Beach was part of the hippie culture. In a sense, it has not changed all that much. Famous people like Jim Morrison, the late front man from the musical group "The Doors," joined the hippie scene in Venice Beach in 1965. For Doors and Morrison fans like my sister Debbie Bucking, who visited me with my nephew Paul Michael this summer, there is a huge mural of Morrison painted on an apartment building wall at 1811 Speedway Avenue. As for the legend Morrison, "the majority of the Doors gigs were played at the Cheetah on the pier" (Beverly Hills Rent-A-Car, 2008).

Venice Beach was a perfect place for people like Morrison to blend in. In the '60s young people came to Venice to smoke pot, use other drugs like acid or LSD, which is reported to have been legal to purchase at the head shops on the beach in the 60s, as the "Captain of Venice" will explain in detail when we interview him. Many head shops still exist today, as do the pot smokers who hold up signs that read, "Will work 4 Marijuana" or yell out, "Need weed for medical research."

As we observe the police walking the beat, they do nothing in response to people holding up their signs because the people are exercising their First Amendment right to free speech. The man with the marijuana sign was a homeless man in his 30s, long blonde hair, wearing jeans and no shirt, sitting on the pavement, legs crossed, with all of his life belongings sitting behind him in a basket. He is a sight!

The Ocean Front Walk was built in 1972. At that time there was nude sunbathing, which gained national media attention, and there was rebellion. When big money investors bought into Venice, the average family in Venice felt they had just as much right to live on Venice Beach as the rich. They were in an uproar over just whom the beach belonged to.

Venice Beach gained further notoriety in 1975 when current California governor Arnold Schwarzenegger, the seven-time Mr. Olympia, trained at Gold's Gym in Santa Monica and Venice Beach under the guidance of renowned body-builder Joe Weider. Schwarzenegger, his friend Franco Columbo, and other famous bodybuilders also contributed to making this place a world-known monument to bodybuilders and tourists from around the world. For athletes and body builders alike, you may remember the famous movie *Pumping Iron,* which was filmed at Gold's Gym in Venice. This movie made Schwarzenegger into an international movie star. In fact, on July 4, Franco Columbo visited Muscle Beach as he was to be inducted into the Hall of Fame at Venice Beach. Franco, although overweight, showed his strength by blowing up a hot water bottle like a balloon until it popped.

I was talking to one local old timer Jimmy Mecham who said that the late former All-Pro football star Lyle Alzado was known to occasionally work out on Muscle Beach when he played for the Los Angeles Raiders. He would often show off his muscle mass by walking the beach on his hands and prior to the '60s and '70s, fitness pioneer Jack La Lane displayed his natural physical prowess on Muscle Beach.

For today's muscle-heads out there visiting Venice, Muscle Beach still has its magic because it has earned its place in history. Today, Muscle Beach is a tourist attraction without the famous people. You do occasionally see the walking steroid hitting the beach or walkway to show off the drug-induced muscles, which have an impact on those who are obsessed with the look.

In 1984, Venice Beach tourism was at its peak with the Olympics Games being held in Los Angeles. There was a great deal of television coverage, which showed why Venice Beach is one of the greatest spots for tourists from around the globe. Athletes from all over the world visited during the Games, and the Olympic Marathon was held nearby our apartment just one block from the beach on Pacific Avenue, which runs straight into Santa Monica.

The dark side of Venice Beach emerged in the 1990s when Venice Beach reportedly became a consortium for inner-city gangs. On a hot summer afternoon, "up to 2,000 thugs gathered on the beach. After some problems with the 'gangsta' mentality, the word was out that Venice was turned into a gang playground and as a result, tourism declined" (LA Conservancy).

In Los Angeles in 1991, residents have a greater chance of dying from a bullet wound than from a car accident. Murders averaged four per day. Rapes, assaults, and other violent felonies were also on the rise.

In 1998, a $10,000,000 bond issue was passed to refurbish Venice Beach's recreation facilities.

Venice Beach was also a favorite place to visit for the late president of the United States, Ronald Reagan. An article that *CNN* published on June 5, 2005 states, "The former Hollywood film actor stopped going to his Century City office in 1999, but still made trips to parks and enjoyed strolls on the Venice Beach boardwalk with his Secret Service contingent" (CNN, 2004).

Today, Venice Beach is known as the "Mecca for Free Expression" because artists from all over the planet share and market their talent to the masses of tourists who visit the beach community each year.

This is the second year we have rented an apartment suite on Rose Avenue, which is owned by Dick Neal, whose mother Helen purchased the home from Abbott Kinney in the mid 1900s. We had the opportunity to meet Neal's great grandnephew Sam Cook, whose mother is the sister of New York Yankees great and Hall of Fame player Bill Dickey. That makes Sam the baseball great Bill Dickey's nephew.

There is Venice Beach, and then there is the rest of the world. Venice Beach is an experience! Countless movies and hundreds of television shows use Venice to film, including its beach and pier, the canals, boardwalk, and Venice High School. Rose Avenue is an exciting place for the entertainment industry. It acts as a hub for Hollywood because of its historic relevance, prime location, and proximity to Venice Beach, which is less than one hundred yards away. In our apartment building on Rose, episodes for a reality television sitcom for Tufts Movie Channel were filmed in the apartment lobby.

We watched the *Food Network* and MTV's *Next* film directly outside our apartment. In addition to its beautiful canals and beaches, Venice Beach has a flavor of a bohemian residential area as well as a feeling that you don't get anywhere else.

The local communities in the beachfront area of Venice have a diverse population of people, a strong economic climate, and a mixture of both low- and high-end businesses where the upper and middle class coexist with the homeless. California is one of the most expensive places to live in the country. In fact, in a May 7, 2006 article in the *New York Times* titled "The Least Affordable Place to Live? Try Salinas," Alina Tugend wrote, "California has the distinction of having the 11 least-affordable metropolitan areas in the country. One would need to go all the way down to 12th place and across the country to the New York region's northern suburbs to find a non-California metropolitan area on the least-affordable list of 2005" (New York Times, 2006).

Affordability is not a concept on a homeless person's mind. The homeless simply fight for survival and are not concerned about statistics like these. To them, statistics are trivial. The homeless I interviewed care about their day-to-day existence, not how they could buy a home and move out of the poverty category on a W-2 Form.

While money is being poured into the community, the homeless problem remains unsolved. Many of the buildings on Venice Beach and the surrounding community are old and need improvements. A contingency plan would help to maintain the positive image for tourists as well. The plan should be one committed to serving the public's best interest and it should include an improvement and follow-up plan whereby the quality of life for the helpless, hopeless, and homeless population improves towards being more productive.

Just because people are homeless, it should not mean that they lose their voice in finding solutions to Venice Beach's problems. Many of the high-functioning homeless people are extremely intelligent and would be willing to participate in a roundtable discussion on any topic that improves the water or environment or quality of life here in Venice Beach.

My favorite place to stay is the incredible Venice Suites on the beach next to the Cadillac Hotel. Randy runs a gorgeous, friendly complex where you can mingle with people from all over the world. All this and so much more are packed onto Venice Beach.

It would be interesting if we could bring Abbott Kinney back and listen to his thoughts on the Venice scene today. He would most likely cherish much of what he saw, but I wonder if he ever imagined the countless number of homeless who live here in this paradise.

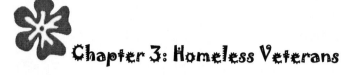

Chapter 3: Homeless Veterans

Inspired by War Veterans with Post-Traumatic Stress Disorder

Pruitt: "Home of the Free!"

Photo: David Dickinson

Former Suffolk Community College Student Corey Morgan delivers his dramatic interpretation of a wounded Vietnam Veteran to homeless Pruitt, wounded in action in 1965 losing his arm in the war, and his comrades. Author Bill O'Connell (left) seated with Pruitt (Right).

The first time I visited Venice Beach was in April 2004. I had some free time while traveling with students from Suffolk County

Community College, Grant Campus, in Brentwood, New York, where I teach a number of classes. At the time, I was the co-director of the speech and debate team that competed in the Phi Rho Pi National Speech and Debate Tournament for two-year junior colleges held in Woodland Hills, California, when we decided to visit Venice Beach.

That day, another veteran, a person I had never met before, gave us all a new appreciation for the people who serve this country. He inspired me to write this book. I can still recall the look in his eyes and the passion he had in telling us his story. While he may not have been able to stand the face he sees in the mirror, he made a very positive impression that will be forever etched in my mind. This experience elevated my own personal ambitions in the spirit of the American Flag and all veterans become a memorial illuminated by the thought of red, white, and blue and its patriotic meaning.

It was here on Venice Beach that I had my first communication experience with homeless people, and it was here that I would live for the next four summers, interviewing, studying, researching, and observing both day and night. The experience was humbling then, and it is even more humbling now. After exposure to a Vietnam War veteran on the beach and watching homeless people eat from garbage pails, I guess you can say I had a "revelation" and decided to share my uncommon perspective on the methods I used to talk to homeless people who are dislocated from society.

Most people take umbrage at the homeless, but I walked right up to a man sitting on a bench near the central area of Venice Beach between Washington Avenue and Rose Avenue, just before world-famous Muscle Beach, to see what he was selling. The man introduced himself as "Pruitt." He spoke in a soft voice with a distinctive California accent and a touch of Louisiana drawl. Pruitt was a homeless Vietnam veteran. He was wearing a leather jacket over his worn military jacket. He had on a bandana and a hat, and had a scruffy beard and wrinkled skin. He looked like a throwback from the '60s in his war attire, and had the American flag draped over a box that he used to sell war memorabilia, such as the American flag, bald eagle, and stickers of the flag. This was no ordinary homeless person trying to make an income or send a message, or was he?

Looking at Pruitt, I thought that in many ways the homeless are treated the way Vietnam veterans in this country were treated in the '60s and '70s when they were not welcomed home by the very country they defended. I remember when I was a child how this unpopular view affected one of my friends where I attended Catholic school. His father had spent eight years as a prisoner of war in Vietnam. The perception people had of his father was that he was a weirdo, a nut, a crazy Vietnam veteran who would be a danger to the community because of his psychological problems from being tortured in Vietnam.

Kids used to make fun of my friend because they said his father was a murderer who killed innocent people, when in fact he was an Air

Force Special Forces operator shot down in combat and captured early in the war.

After saying hello and initiating a conversation with Pruitt, we did not want to unnerve him, but we asked him if he was homeless, to which he replied, "Yes." He appeared friendly, so I asked him if he would mind sharing his perspective on life so that my students and I could get a better understanding of what it is like to live homeless. Pruitt said, "Are you sure?" I insisted. Pruitt then began by telling us the painful memory of how he had lost his left arm while serving his country in Vietnam. His story made a profound impact on me.

The draft for Vietnam ended in 1973, but for a man named Pruitt, it seemed liked yesterday as he relived the story that many veterans live in their minds nearly every minute of the day.

December 1, 1969 marked the date of the first draft lottery held in the United States since 1942. Pruitt's story began on a warm June day in 1969 shortly after he graduated from high school. He had written his last English essay on "the essence of life" in which he wrote about his dreams and aspirations and how he planned to help make a difference in the world. His mother, Rachel, was a woman who deeply cared about her son. She was concerned about a different issue in the country, one that her young graduating son did not yet fully understand, the Vietnam conflict. Weeks after graduating from high school, Pruitt walked in the door of his two-story home in Baton Rouge, Louisiana and he called out to his mother to let her know that he was home.

There was no response from above, but he knew that his mother was home because her car was in the driveway. Suddenly, footsteps coming down the stairs tapped like a noise he had never heard his mother make before. The steps were rapid and heavy, but there were no words spoken. Pruitt said he looked in his mother's eyes and was saying, "How come you are not answering me, Mom?" His mother was carrying an opened envelope from the Selective Service System that read "Order to Report for Armed Forces Physical Exam," which meant that Pruitt was called to serve the United States in Vietnam. Pruitt kept asking his mother, "Momma, why aren't you saying anything to me, what's wrong with you?" Finally, his mother replied, crying, "I have been trying to find a way to hide this from you, this letter, and I know I should not have opened this letter because it is addressed to you, but you have been drafted to serve in Vietnam."

In his state of innocence, Pruitt said he felt a sense of confusion as to what serving in Vietnam meant, and as he got up from his chair to hug his mother, he told her that everything would be okay and there was nothing to worry about. His mother was very distraught over the fact that she might never see her son again. Initially, Pruitt felt angry, and then as if he was cheated. He was cheated out of life and possibly his future, but he did his best to maintain his composure so that his mother would not be too upset. When Pruitt was told where to report for his physical and what the process would entail, he abided.

Within months, he was on a C-130 overlooking the ocean and Vietnam's canopy of mountains and jungle as his plane landed fully loaded with Marines in Saigon. Pruitt thought back to that pivotal time in his life:

"I will never forget looking into the eyes of my fellow Marines, now fully aware that we were trained to kill people and take away human life. Shit, just looking back at writing that last essay for my high school English class, all I could think was, what the hell would I write now? My whole life was about to change. As we were landing I could see beautiful palm trees which from inside of a plane looked very inviting. The platoon leader yelled out as we landed on the tarmac, 'Get your gear ready, we are unloading and visiting Disneyland.'"

The fully loaded plane was filled with men who would become what we know today as Vietnam combat veterans. Some of the men would be killed never to see their families again, some would become heroes saving fellow soldiers, and some would go home severely wounded, but nearly all who saw combat would go home forever after dealing with the daily trauma of war.

Pruitt reflected, "The second that back door opened from the C-130, all I could feel was numbness. It was one hundred degrees with humidity and the scent of jet fuel didn't help me

27

to breathe any better. I wanted to die right here, but then my peers would have thought I was a coward. I was only eighteen years old. I looked across the way at another plane being loaded. Its cargo was the caskets from my fallen comrades. They seemed to number by the dozens. It was not the way I thought I would begin my tour in Vietnam, but I am sure I was not alone in fear. I wanted to cry, and I did inside, but I wanted to survive too. I just did not know how to yet. My image was of my casket being sent back to my mother to bury."

Weeks later the time came for Pruitt's platoon to take care of business and hunt the enemy. It was the government's enemy, not Pruitt's. Actually, Pruitt made it clear that his fight was to survive and if it meant he had to kill, then that was the way it was.

The first few weeks, Pruitt did not see much action. They heard a few machine-gun shots and mortar rounds here and there, but his platoon received no direct fire for the first few encounters with the Viet Cong. Call it the lottery system, but each Marine learns how to take point until he is mentored enough to lead a walk. Pruitt said, "I was with my platoon that consisted of about twenty men, just before Thanksgiving in 1969, when we were dropped from our Huey helicopter, armed with rockets and a .30-caliber machine gun, into the open canopy and jungle terrain of Vietnam."

He continued, "To me, Vietnam was unique from other wars in that we had trouble separating the good from the bad people, you see. Some of the bad guys were little kids with grenades, ready to sacrifice their lives for their cause. We had a firebase which was usually the only secure or safe area, and boy did I miss that firebase when we had to go out on patrol. The rest of the field or jungle belonged to the enemy or 'Charlie,' which stands for the Viet Cong or VC. The hardliner enemy could be found between a place called Chu Lai and Da Nang, north to the Demilitarized Zone, and east/west from the South China Sea.

They didn't teach us anything about Vietnam in high school and I was too naïve to realize that I would be at the center of this conflict far away from home where the green grass of the baseball field seemed like just a fantasy and pipe dream.

It was my turn to take point during a tactical operation while carrying my M-16. You see, when a soldier takes point, it is his responsibility to guide the troops to safety, find trip wires and land mines, and hunt and kill the enemy. We operated in sixteen-foot-high elephant grass and one-hundred-degree temperature where the humidity buried us in sweat, and we had to lather up with no-scent tanning lotion to protect our skin. Shit, man, Venice is freezing in comparison! I also carried my .45-caliber pistol, three or four clips of ammunition, six fragment grenades, six smoke grenades, a compass, maps, and a poncho, but my brother, [smiling] I tell you, I was fucking scared to death, literally pissing in my pants, eighteen year old walking through the jungles of Vietnam with no fucking mama around to make my bed. But I was also a proud serving member of the Marines, a grunt."

When asked if he could remember what went through his head while on point, he shouted as though reliving this memory was becoming more painful,

"Do you have any fucking idea how scared I was? I was so numb, but focused fearing for my life, and there was no time to dope up with that killer marijuana out in the jungle that everyone was smoking to help hide that fear. So, I thought about my mom, who I had reason to live for, Dad who died when I was eleven, my two brothers and sister, and my girlfriend who I missed so much, but fuck, I knew I needed to survive and fight for my life."

The eyes of my students zoomed in on Pruitt's mouth as they hung on every word he said. Pruitt continued,

"We followed our orders to scope out the location and kill the enemy that day, but unfortunately in a matter of a second, the fucking jungle came alive and my life flashed in front of me. I stepped on the trip wire to a booby trap, which was hooked up to a tree. The trap is called a 'Punji' or Bamboo Whip, which was attached to a tree lined with razor-sharp bamboo blades. The VC generally used Punji pits to kill or trap animals, but in this case, they hung the log from a tree and once you were unfortunate enough to trip the trap, it swung from the tree and could easily kill a man, especially if it hit you in the chest. Just seconds before I was hit with the whip, my platoon leader yelled, "Watch the tripwires, asshole." That one second of warning saved my life, but every day I think of that second as though it is the only second I have lived my life. That fucking second… [tears], it is like a second that has become frozen in time in my life. The fucking log hit me so hard, it sliced my arm in half as it dangled in front of me. It hit me with the force of what felt like a small car, but with the blades. As I looked to my left I watched my friend Johnny's twenty-one-year-old face and skull blown off by an incoming AK-47 machine gun round, which killed him instantly as his guts splattered on me. It all happened so fast and I was screaming at the top of my lungs. My brothers in the platoon started shooting wild, but other people were dropping all around me from the incoming small-arms fire. At the time, we did not know it, but we walked into the 'kill-zone' of an enemy ambush by a small unit of VC. I cared more about my team than my arm. As I lay in blood, three of my friends were mortally wounded and I could see my other friend to my direct right, Mickey's body bubble up and down from the Rocket-Propelled Grenade (RPG) that just pierced his chest as blood flew out like a volcano erupting like the devil. I watched him breathe his last breath of life. There was blood, blood, and more blood everywhere. That disaster combined with the smell of death and burning bodies from incoming mortar rounds and RPGs is something that I have not been able to overcome in my life. That day, three of my best friends were killed and five others were wounded out of the twenty men with us. It was a different world, my friend."

Pruitt said we brought him back to the most painful time in his life, but he still recalls the campfire discussions they had before operating the next day they went into battle. He said his platoon feared talking about death and hid the fear by using drugs, mostly marijuana. He explained how the drug masked the paranoia of soldiers before the storm of violence and destruction of human life war brings.

I tried to relate Pruitt's story to some that my father had told me. He had seen a lot working for the Emergency Service Unit and SWAT team with the New York City Police Department, but I found Pruitt's story to be one of the most compelling and moving stories I have ever heard. My young eighteen- to twenty-year-old students were speech-less. Pruitt made us feel as though we were there with him, trying to win back the lives of the dead comrades that were lost on foreign turf to a determined enemy.

Pruitt said that he had never heard men scream so loudly and the screams are haunting. He said that before he was drafted as a soldier, he was a happy teenager. He had intentions to go to college and become a baseball player, where he thought that as an outfielder, he could make it to the minors. When his arm was destroyed, so were his dreams.

He said, "I never imagined my life turning out this way. Even on the long plane ride to the other side of the world, I thought to myself, Vietnam is bigger then me, this is bigger than my life. I am not man enough to face a war, I am too young, but I have no choice. In Vietnam, I thought I was going to be like a police officer protecting the South Vietnamese. When I heard reports that some of my friends from my home-town of Baton Rouge, Louisiana came home in body bags I think I was in denial that this would become an all-out war. I didn't learn how to shoot and kill someone, nor did I ever think I would have to. I wish I went to college, but I lost all desire af-ter the Vietnam War. It was as if lighting struck and drained every ounce of life out of me. I need no sympathy. I would still fight and die for my country today."

I asked Pruitt how it felt coming home to a country that did not support the war. He said, "I find that people had compassion to an extent, but I honestly feel that people forget the fallen heroes of Vietnam and the war because it was a war that this country doesn't want to remember. Regardless of what the war did to our country, I am a proud United States Marine, thank you for listening," he finished.

As fate would have it, Corey Morgan was there that day. Corey was one of the best competitors on our speech and debate team. We made eye contact with each other and looked to Pruitt, who was seated, and we knew that the veteran was in for a memorable and unforgettable treat. The moment had me feeling the sense that everything in this world happens for a reason as the magnificent connection between two strangers, Morgan and Pruitt, left us all feeling the energy of the moment. Days like this are memorable!

Morgan has won countless trophies competing at the junior-college level in Dramatic Interpretation events in speech and debate tournaments. He has a favorite motto, "God Bless America."

Morgan has his own act on Vietnam, and after a little encouragement from Junior College All-American David Dickinson and me, Morgan agreed to deliver his oral interpretation rendition of a Vietnam veteran who returned home from the war in Vietnam with his face distorted from an explosive, which detonated in his face. Pruitt later recounted that that faceless-soldier story Corey delivered reminded him of what his friend could have been had he survived the shot from the AK-47. The piece is about ten minutes long, but Morgan gave a three- to four-minute teaser of the most powerful and emotional part of the act. For Pruitt, it was a spiritual moment, as if a higher power brought us all together for that exact time on this sixty-degree day with little rays of sunshine stretching through the clouds. We were all caught up in a different moment in time.

Morgan captivated Pruitt as he delivered his moving and highly emotional act, which brought Pruitt to tears. I was crying too. The veteran rose from his seat, saluted Morgan with his remaining limb, and then thanked Morgan for bringing something meaningful to his day. Morgan's performance brought meaning to everyone's day, especially the homeless war-torn veteran who lives each day with the memory and emotion of losing his fallen comrades. Pruitt then turned to me and handed me an American flag bandana, which I wear for the photo on the back cover of this book, as his blue eyes met mine. "Take this flag and never forget my friends Johnny and Mickey, and all veterans who died for the beautiful U S of A," he said. This precious moment left a connection between the academic world and the spirit of humanity that Pruitt shared in his reality. It was as though it was Veterans Appreciation Day. Pruitt lives in hell every day, thinking about the friends he lost nearly forty years ago. He knows he cannot take back the consequences of that day, but his reality dictates his choice to be homeless, especially after telling us that his mother died of a heart attack in 1970. The rest of his family went their own way and made lives for themselves.

Pruitt said that life is filled with struggles and those struggles have created a minefield of obstacles that prevent him from healing. In a sense, Pruitt has died as an individual. Pruitt is not alone. Veterans represent a large portion of the homeless.

On the other end of the spectrum, my friend and colleague Lars Hedstrom, Professor of Communication at Suffolk County Community College, Ammerman Campus, was a Special Forces Operator in Vietnam who saw more than the average servicemen. I asked him what his experience was in the Vietnam War to try to compare to that of Pruitt's.

He said, "I killed my share of 'gooks,' saw people blown to ashes right in front of me…An incoming mortar round explodes and I'm blown backwards off my feet not a scratch, but the kid I was talking to—GONE. In mid-sentence…he's an unrecognizable heap of 'red stuff.' I held a young soldier in my arms as he took his last breath. His last word was 'Mom'…I shit you not!

But one 'kill' hasn't ever left me. While on patrol with the 4th Infantry, I remember looking up suddenly and unexpectedly I looked into the eyes of a VC, not five feet from me, half-assed hidden in a hole. He had me in his rifle sights—dead to rights. I heard his weapon's bolt go forward and I froze, held my breath calmly expecting to die, but his AK jammed. In the time it took to exhale, I tore him up...fired a full AR-15 magazine into his face. I stood there for only a few moments...heard him scream—strange sounds coming from somewhere in that twisted mass of ripped-open flesh. I could smell the scent of his blood in the air. I watched him slowly slump down, moaning. He was done. It seemed that simple at that moment. But I knew AKs never jammed. I picked up his weapon. The trigger had been pulled. Somehow two rounds had been simultaneously stripped from the magazine. The bolt couldn't close and lock. The firing pin couldn't strike and fire a partially chambered round. I tossed the rifle down into the hole on top of the body I had just killed and kept walking as if nothing special had just happened. A few angry seconds, I lived—he didn't.

If the topic is post-traumatic stress, I was lucky. I don't believe I was or ever will be affected. I volunteered for combat duty. I was well trained prior to going to RVN. I didn't have time to dwell on the past. After a tour with the 4th Infantry in '66 to '67, I stayed in the service, returned to my previous duty station: Army Ranger Training Command, Fort Benning, Georgia. Special Forces School followed, then 'classified'

Special Operations based out of Okinawa throughout Southeast Asia till 1973. I was a pro."

Both of these patriotic men love their country. The difference between Pruitt and Lars is immeasurable with one finding grief in being drafted to fight in the war losing his arm and sense of purpose, and the other, volunteering to fight and ultimately finding a way to channel a level of positive energy, enough to propel him to where he makes every minute count in a life, a life filled with accomplishments.

 Chapter 4

Murder on the Beach

Photo: William G. O'Connell
An unknown golfer swings away just steps in front of the exact spot where Coby McBee lost his life as the gorgeous Malibu Mountains peek through the Venice Beach palm trees in the distance.

Going from an education environment where I just finished teaching my summer session class and enjoying the students in it, I moved on to a different environment, Venice Beach again, where anything goes. Normally, people don't go around trying to engage homeless people, but that's what makes me different. Although I can't say that I have lived homeless, observing and interacting with them day and night, I have a very good idea of how they go about surviving and know that if I had to live as a homeless person, I could survive. Living homeless could mean that you eat from garbage pails, pick up cigarettes from the pavement, and at times beg for money, clothes, food, and other necessities. And then there are many categories of homeless: homeless by choice or design; homeless due to mental illness; homeless due to loss of foreclosure, home, and job; homeless due to drugs and alcohol; homeless due to domestic violence; homeless Vietnam and Iraqi War veterans; but the most dangerous are the criminal homeless released from prison, who may have assaulted someone or spent hard time previously. On Venice, the homeless travel solo and at times in groups. The groups are usually camped out and circled around a comfortable palm tree under the shade. How do I know? I simply got to know many of them in the summers when I lived here to observe them.

After spending a period of time in a community, people get to know each other well. Combing the beach gave us the opportunity to recognize the behaviors of people in the day and evening hours, and since we operated in both, we made lots of acquaintances. Some of the homeless we met slept during the day and showed up at night.

After our first visit to Venice Beach and after being compelled to write a book about the homeless, my partner Jane and I found ourselves looking out our window as we awakened to a gorgeous blue sky, with the California sunshine reflecting on our balcony above Rose Avenue overlooking the Pacific Ocean.

On this particular morning, as we walked out onto our balcony with a pair of high-powered binoculars, we saw surfers riding four- to six-foot waves in the ocean while schools of dolphins hurtled playfully through the water with their young. There were bikers and skaters gliding by on the boardwalk as the unmistakable scent of bacon and eggs from the restaurant across the street filled the ocean air. Suddenly, in the public parking lot below, two unmarked cars pulled into the empty lot and four anxious-looking plainclothes Los Angeles Police Department detectives with badges and weapons attached to their waists stepped out of the cars. They engaged in an intense interview with a man who slowly walked up to the car. I recognized the man that the detectives met with as one of the homeless who lives on the beach under a Hawaiian umbrella with his son. His unmistakable long hair, jeans, grubby beard, and checkered brown and grey flannel shirt stood out as the meeting went on for twenty minutes, until the detectives and the man went their separate ways.

Being inquisitive is a prerequisite when writing a book, but on Venice Beach, people don't take too kindly to nosy authors who ask too many questions. The next day, on the Walk, we overheard some of the locals talking about the recent "transient" murder, but information was vague at best.

After asking a few people questions about the murder, and about the person who may have been killed, we came up empty. We watched the news on television and searched the LAPD web site for the Venice Pacific Division, which is responsible for the beach territory near the Venice Pier, to see if there was information regarding these murders, but we found nothing.

Three days later, on July 27, *The Argonaut, Venice Forum Newspaper* of Los Angeles reported that a thirty-six-year-old homeless man was stabbed to death during what police described as "a dispute between two transients near the Venice Beach Boardwalk, Thursday, July 20th" (The Argonaut, 2006). Five months earlier, in a February 16 article titled, "Murder of Venice Homeless Goes Unnoticed," the same source and author reported that "there have reportedly been 12 homeless women murdered in the last few years in Venice Beach – and this never hit the news" (The Argonaut, 2006).

In fact, LAPD COMPSTAT Citywide Profile released their July 29th update that 274 homicides in Los Angeles occurred in 2006, down 7 percent from 2005. The police newsroom reported no transient Venice Beach murder, but they did report more than "17,000 violent crimes, 520 rapes, 8,210 robberies, and an alarming 8,323 aggravated assaults" committed in Los Angeles in 2006 (LAPD COMPSTAT, 2006).

The simple fact is, there wouldn't be hate crimes against homeless people if homelessness did not exist. Living on the streets increases the chances of encountering violence, and in LA with those statistics, the chances are better than good. These crimes affect all of us. In this country "there have been more than 770 attacks against homeless that have been documented. Crimes range from golf club beatings to setting a homeless man on fire. The age range of the victims which include Veterans, men, women, and children is four months to seventy-four years old" (National Homeless.Org, 2008).

What about the other murders that were reported, I thought.

Less than a month after the murder, when I contacted the LAPD Media Relations Bureau by phone, I was finally able to learn the victim's name. A source in the police department provided a name for the thirty-six-year-old homeless man who was murdered: Coby McBee. However, the police would not provide me with a last known address or any other information for McBee. Police also claimed that only four people were murdered in the past two years on the beach, not twelve. Three people died from gunshot wounds on Main Street and South Venice Boulevard, while one person was beaten to death on Market Street in Venice on April 30, 2005 (LAPD FOIA Crime Data, 2006). This directly contradicts *The Argonaut Forum Newspaper's* February 16 story.

The little bit of information about McBee that the LAPD provided through the Freedom of Information Act was not enough for me to understand all the details of the murder, but it did open a discovery trail. I decided to take a different approach by reaching out to one of many of my New York City Police Department contacts, who managed to provide me with McBee's last known address, his mother's telephone number, and everything I needed to put a face and a life to the name.

Before I picked up the phone to call McBee's mother, I had many questions running through my head: "What do I say? How do I act? When do I end the conversation?" Most important, since the reality of the situation was that my intent was to tell a story to a reader based on a murdered person, I did not know how Mrs. McBee would react. I thought the worst, fearing she would not be interested in her son's story being out there, but I was wrong.

I dialed Mrs. McBee's number and left a message on her answering machine. That evening, my phone rang, and it was Coby McBee's mother, Kathryn, who lives in St. Joseph, Missouri.

At first, I could not measure the value of the conversation, but I found in talking to Mrs. McBee that all of these questions came naturally to be answered because she had a way of making me feel comfortable by thanking me right up front for my call before I even asked any questions, making it easier for me. Mrs. McBee has a great personality. She is warm, compassionate, and everything an interviewer could hope for under the circumstances. In retrospect, I felt privileged to serve as one more person who will remember Coby long after his death. Too often, the media forgets the victims and their families.

A Parent's Worst Nightmare

In a shaky, deep, but sweet and raspy voice, Coby McBee's sixty-one-year-old mother said to me, through tears, "Now about Coby, I miss him so bad I can hardly stand it. I now know what it feels like to lose a child. The hurt is so deep and I feel so bad."

McBee's mother continued, "My Coby would not hurt anyone unless it was to defend his family, friends, or if he was provoked. I was told he was defending the honor of a woman, and was stabbed in the chest by a homeless man in his 30s and died shortly after. I wasn't there, but I believe the only way Coby could have been murdered was if he was tired, hungry, and in pain."

The details of the night of the murder at this point are that Coby was with a female acquaintance and in the heat of an exchange between another homeless man, Coby defended the woman whom the other man was yelling at and the exchange became a violent fight, resulting in Coby's being stabbed and murdered. Coby stepped into harm's way to protect his friend. His mother said, referring to his defending himself and why he went to Venice, "He wanted to go all the way and get his black belt. I wish he had never worked for the Drug Strike Force." The Drug Strike Force is a federally funded enhancing interagency which coordinates intelligence and facilitates multi-jurisdictional investigations that target drug and gang crime. Nationwide the Task Force in 2003 "arrested 42,122 suspects and convicted

20,685 offenders. The estimated value of all assets seized was $26,457,556" (OCJP, 2003). In 2008 these numbers continue to climb.

Mrs. McBee said that Coby had moved to California from Missouri in 2004. What led up to Coby's leaving Missouri was his involvement against drugs and drug dealers. To protect his mother, I am not at liberty to expand further on the extent of his involvement, but I will say that Coby left the state knowing that a few bad people would be off the streets, and he was allegedly involved with an undercover operation that netted a few known drug offenders. To escape the pressure of his involvement with the Drug Task Force in his hometown where he played a role in the counterintelligence program, he decided to change the scenery and head in a different direction farther west.

It is a parent's worst nightmare to lose a child.

Mrs. McBee continued, "My Coby loved life. In fact, Coby told me he was afraid to die because he did not want to leave his children without a father." By all indications, he was a person who did his best with what he had and he was systematic in the way he lived his life, but apparently lost his confidence in himself at some point, which can be the signpost to enhancement or the gateway to insecurity. He left behind two children.

Coby's mother, like all parents who lose a child, just wants her son back. She said, "He would still be home safe with his children." In trying to make sense of her son's life and death, Coby's mother was devastated. She said, "I remember my other son showing up from Wichita,

Kansas to inform me of Coby's death, and I just can't accept the fact that he is gone." She still has this image of her son walking through the door. "Coby was precious; he's my baby," said his mother. The last time she spoke to her son was in June, a month prior to his murder. He was murdered near the Market on Dudley, in Venice. That is most likely where his last correspondence came from. In fact, the store's owner on Dudley, Shyla, knew Coby and spoke well of him. Shyla said Coby was a regular visitor to her store and he was able to use the computer frequently.

While he did not set out to be homeless, he did set out to discover what California had to offer. Mrs. McBee said, "Coby sold enough of his stuff and was ready and very excited; he was like a little boy going on an adventure he never thought was possible. He left here in February 2004, with his van fully loaded. It even had a sink in it." That van was subsequently abandoned when Coby's tires were flattened because he parked in a prohibited space. His mother said, "Coby stayed in contact with us faithfully. The road was rough and rocky; he had good times, and he had bad times."

Coby's also studied Hap Ki Do karate, a Korean form of martial arts. The Hap Ki Do of today is a form of unarmed self-defense, and Coby had earned his brown belt with a red tip. Coby was also a very talented musician. His favorite instrument was the keyboard. He was another soul who enjoyed the "free zone" for artistic expression that the Venice Beach environment provides.

Mrs. McBee said, "If I would have taken care of my own business and had my head together, I would have called the coroner and the LAPD and asked what happened." Coby's mother passed that task along to family members, and perhaps the gruesome details were too painful for them to share with her. She said, "I know nothing except what they told me."

When something big happens on Venice Beach, word travels fast. In comparison to a dangerous city like New Orleans, Louisiana where homicides rank amongst the highest numbers in the nation in the aftermath of Hurricane Katrina, Venice Beach is a peaceful place. Like any other suburb in a major city though, it has its problems and there is certainly crime. If you look for it, trouble can find you anywhere in America.

Coby McBee was a brother, father, and son, and regardless of the choices he made in life, he was a kind and gentle human being according to his mother and others. A local business owner who knew Coby told me that he was a considerate man who was always polite when he came into his store. In reality, we cannot take homeless people, shove them in a closet, and pretend they do not exist in this country. Each person represents American culture.

I kept a murdered man and his family in my thoughts and prayers throughout the night.

A year and nine days after Coby McBee was murdered, being persistent, I stopped two members of the Los Angeles Police Department's 9,100-person police force on Brook Street, a few blocks from where Coby McBee was murdered. We had an informative conversation as I asked them how they felt about the homeless living here. They told me sarcastically that aside from the homeless using the beach as a place to go to the bathroom, they really have no problems with them. I then asked the sergeant about last year's murder, referring to Coby McBee. At first, the officer did not recall the McBee murder. As for crime here on Venice Beach, police say they see a lot of theft, but that the beat is generally very safe.

After I explained in detail the information about the McBee case and how I had been talking to his mother, the police officers suddenly seemed to remember the case. I found it odd that although the officers were veterans of the beach, when I did mention the murder they said they did not know about it. Nevertheless, the officers did not seem alarmed by my questions and they did not have any details to offer about McBee either, but they did express sympathy for the McBee family.

Upon telling the officers I was from New York, the officers explained that New York is as diverse as Los Angeles, but there are so many more people in New York by comparison. New York City has one of the largest police forces in the country with more than thirty-two thousand members.

Making communities safe across America takes open dialogue between the community and police in order to cross the barriers that divide. My initial vibe toward the police in Los Angeles changed when I realized that police could also bring about a positive change by showing they genuinely care about people and not just policing. Really, it comes down to communication working as a system to ensure that there is a process in place to help the community to better understand the job of the police; and vice versa, the police need to improve their communication and listening skills in working through the public. I actually proposed one such course at Suffolk Community College, Grant Campus titled "Public Communication in Law Enforcement"; the course focuses on building and maintaining productive and positive relationships in a variety of law enforcement, work, and social settings. We can all play a role in creating harmony in our community.

Coby's personal choices and the risk of going to California were not something his mother thought would cost him his life. In fact, because of his involvement helping the DTF, he was in more danger in Missouri than in California.

For Kathryn McBee, her goal is to simply get through each day, as she recalls everything about her son from his childhood to the day she last saw the smile on his face.

As Coby McBee became another unfortunate police statistic in Los Angeles County for 2006, this book can help to identify the rationale behind his leaving Missouri for California. Through the words of his mother Kathryn, it also helps his children to understand that he was a caring person who had dreams and aspirations just like any other citizen. Any mother wants the best for her children.

Chapter 5

Explanation of the "Functioning Levels" of Homelessness

When dealing with a population that you know little about, you never know what walk of life a person is from or how experiences have shaped a person's vision or attitude toward culture. Understanding these concepts allows a person to dig deeper into the reasons why homeless live the way they do. Because of a homeless woman named Mary, who will be introduced shortly, I had the opportunity to gain the trust of and befriend homeless from the ground floor to the top of the respected homeless chain. By respected, I mean the people within the homeless circle of respect, like the Chief who you will also meet in the forthcoming chapters.

Building positive relationships with strangers is a huge challenge, but after spending what seemed like endless hours with homeless people, using listening and other communication skills, I learned how to be a street smart interviewer so that I could obtain as much information about the homeless as I possibly could. For example, knowing when to back off when someone's tone begins to change is important. At one point when Mary goes into a story about a gang who beat her for her money. Imagine, beating a homeless person for money? Here we have a woman whose false teeth were taken out of her mouth and used to make fun of her by the gang as the gang cut her hair and then slapped her around making her go to an ATM to empty her account of what little she receives from social security income.

In learning more about the homeless, I have found that for the most part this culture lacks the sensitivity that many collective cultures around the world have toward the elderly. Many of the homeless on Venice Beach are elderly. Watching them find their way through the day is completely disheartening. There are also the constantly changing faces of homeless who are younger, mentally ill, drugged out or drug dependent, and aggressive. Each year it becomes evident that the younger and more aggressive type ends up here on the beach, surrounding themselves with homeless dogs, along with hippie-type groups that can be both peaceful and violent.

Homeless people on Venice Beach have their own little community with certain cliques just like mainstream society, only here the game is real because people are trying to survive. Couple with city life with the homeless people who come down to Venice Beach from the tougher sections of Los Angeles, and you have conflict over territory. One night, a man was sleeping in his spot and an older man in his sixties came up and kicked the homeless man while he was sleeping, because he felt the other homeless stranger had taken the space where he slept with his girlfriend. Finally, the younger man got up off the cement and pushed the older man to the ground, and you could hear the sound of his head hitting the ground. The younger man said, "Don't ever touch me again, do you understand?" The older man got up and again started with "Listen, bitch, this is my spot, and it's time to move on, so go, get out of here." He wasn't about to give up that little space. Suddenly, another man came over and decided to lecture the younger man on space, but the drama went on for twenty minutes over a few feet of space until the disagreement was settled with the younger man winning and earning his right to the new piece of real estate.

Then we have a character like Tommy Rock, a well-built man with long blonde hair, homeless more than twenty years, who will plant a mattress on the side of a tight road next to Henry's Market, so close to the road that a car could run the mattress over as he sleeps under the blanket. Tommy is friendly, and as days, nights, weeks, months, and years go by, Tommy changes his place of residence from under the palm tree which he calls "Pole 19," to the streets, as life becomes more dangerous.

Creating functioning levels helps to determine the communication skills of each person. It provides a way to better understand why each individual homeless person does what he or she does.

Trying to track down the same people I interviewed the year before, however, proved to be a challenge each of the last three summers. Some I found, others I did not. Let us just say that for many, life is a struggle, and for the colorful characters in the book—even the best fiction writers could not make this stuff up about the lifestyles that they live.

In the beginning of this venture, I stereotyped the homeless, but I quickly discovered that homelessness covers a vast territory and that many of the stereotypes I held about the homeless were inaccurate. Rather than stereotype further, I thought that it would be best to classify the homeless that I met and interviewed into different levels based on their ability to function on a day-to-day basis. I used three levels: High, Mid- and Low-Functioning.

Oddly enough, there are homeless people who led semi-normal lives before they became homeless. However, most fall victim to life circumstances: war, drug and alcohol abuse or addiction, domestic violence, broken homes, and mental illness. They ran away from their former lives and families and now they are homeless. Some are homeless by design, and others are mentally disturbed, irrational, and sometimes dangerous to themselves and others.

Telling a story about some of the people I met is difficult, especially since most drink, and when they are intoxicated, they sometimes do not make any sense. As a former reporter, I try my best to determine the credibility of a person first in order to decide who is sound enough to interview in depth, while running simple investigations on each person. The hardest part is persuading people to sign a release for an interview and convincing them that their voice matters. I have a way of asking questions that keeps a person engaged in a conversation.

I attempt to tap into their deepest and, at times, most painful and emotional experiences, without their even realizing that they are opening up to me. This process is slow; I use the foot-in-the-door technique I once used as a reporter asking for small bits of information and building up to discovering more about a person.

At times, some of the people I spoke to broke down entirely and cried in my arms. I was also able to connect with many on the most personal level, speaking to their true self, the one hidden down so far inside that they almost forget that it is there. I allow them to express their true selves without fear of judgment or recriminations. I build a relationship using charisma, honesty, and genuine concern for people that they can sense, and therefore they let their guard down and tell me their life stories. Many times, there were no words that could express how I felt about the pain they have endured. I could have easily compared the pain of my son's Bone Marrow Transplant and minimized their reasons for being homeless, but I realized that we all have problems, some more profound than others. What makes their stories interesting is the fact that they live this nomad life, vastly different from our own.

Rather than being part of the problem, it is more useful to find solutions. We all have our own ways of dealing with problems; some rise to the occasion and some spiral down into a world of self-abuse through drugs and alcohol or submit to the crushing tide of depression.

Once we close our minds to understanding, we shut off the learning valve. The fact is, almost anyone can end up homeless. A tragedy, not being able to cope, a loss of a job, being lonely, being mentally ill, total loss of positive self-concept, divorce, drug and alcohol use, and even criminal behavior are consistent themes which can cause a pattern of homelessness.

At the top of the list and hierarchy of homeless are the "High-Functioning" or self-sufficient. These men and women are highly effective, are articulate communicators, and treat all people with respect, including the police. They may also have reached a higher level of education. Some of the High-Functioning and self-sufficient homeless are resourceful and clever enough to generate income by working part-time. High-Functioning homeless are coherent and able to function as well as you or I, and they could easily make it in our world. The difference is they are homeless by design, a subject I will discuss as we go deeper into the book when I introduce Patty. The High-Functioning care very much about their surroundings and are capable of building productive interpersonal relationships with others; whereas the Mid- and Low-Functioning homeless may show indifference, and many are nonconformists, and nearly all show signs of severe social anxiety. High-Functioning homeless can also become Mid-Functioning when they use drugs or alcohol until the point of intoxication.

The next functioning level of homelessness is the "Mid-Functioning" and, at times, socially inept homeless. Whereas the High-

Functioning homeless may not accept food and/or clothes, the Mid-Functioning homeless consist of people who rely heavily on others for food and clothes, but they lack appropriate self-control and interpersonal communication skills, and are more likely to harm themselves and/or others around them. Socially, the Mid-Functioning are only moderately competent and effective communicators, meaning you could have a conversation with them, but they may turn against you if they disagree with you.

The Mid-Functioning homeless are not afraid to commit acts that are unacceptable to society, they are less inhibited, and at times they show no remorse for their conduct. For example, they feel no shame and as a result, they may urinate or remove their clothes in public, use profanities and racial slurs, scream at innocent people and the police, eat from garbage pails, and share a common drinking container or cigarette from the ground. While on the surface they may demonstrate these negative behaviors, if the communication channel opens with Mid-Functioning homeless people, they can be very informative like Mary.

Lastly, the Low-Functioning homeless are perhaps the saddest of the homeless and the most in need. Most lack enough interpersonal and social skills to communicate competently, and in fact, they are poor communicators who may have communication disorders because of mental illness. These people may or may not be willing to accept clothes, food, or money from the public, and oftentimes wear the same clothes for months without washing the clothes or bathing themselves.

Many of the Low-Functioning homeless are introverts. They talk to themselves or imaginary people and want very little interaction with the public. Many are loners who display signs of social anxiety, eat out of garbage pails, and pick things up off the ground like the Mid-Functioning homeless, but the difference is they can sit for hours in one place and they show signs of obsessive compulsive disorder.

Low-Functioning homeless people may also show signs of schizo-phrenia, ramble senselessly and at times display angry conversation that borders on violent behavior, and may inflict harm on themselves or others if you disturb them. Low-Functioning homeless may not be accountable for some of their actions because they suffer from some form of mental disorder that at times can make them irrational. I learned that using caution is very important when dealing with Low-Functioning homeless people because their unpredictability can be harmful.

In California and around the country, many homeless are helpless and mentally disturbed. There are also homeless who we believe practice learned helplessness by accepting money, but are clearly capable of working and are not helpless. The learned helpless appear to be caught in a vicious cycle in which they get locked up for petty offences, and within months of being released, they only find themselves back in jail again for violating the law. Some of these people are capable of putting themselves in a position to both work and clean up their act. Then there are others like the Low-Functioning homeless who are helpless and in desperate need of professional mental health assistance. There is a clear distinction between the two.

The scholarly importance of creating these functioning levels helps us to categorize and find a fair medium and guideline to identify and understand the different levels of homelessness. Just as there are different classes in society, there are different classifications of homelessness. Regardless of the functioning levels, all are homeless yet able to survive in Venice Beach, some better than others.

Many homeless in Venice Beach are from other parts of the country and even other parts of the world. It is important to examine the circumstances that may factor into the choice the homeless make to be here.

 **Chapter 6**

Mary: The Star of the Show

Photo: William G. O'Connell
Mary screams about her life of pain and misery to Jane.

Traveling from New York to Los Angeles for the summer is a relief in many ways. Southern California is the perfect place to reflect on

life while absorbing the peace and intercultural experiences of colorful and bohemian Venice Beach.

I thought that the best way to be productive in my time off for the past three summers would be to write this book so that readers can understand the plight of homelessness in this country through the eyes of the people like Pruitt and Mary, who by nature is precisely the kind of homeless person I want society to understand.

It takes all kinds of people to make this world spin. The most memorable that I met in my time at Venice Beach was a force of nature named Mary. Locals call her "Crazy Mary." Mary herself tells me to call her Crazy Mary, and she can be potentially dangerous to herself and others. Meeting Mary, a fifty-three-year-old homeless woman, for the first time was quite a culture shock for me personally, but she brings a new definition to the word "character." At first glance, Mary appeared to be a Low-Functioning homeless person. She would later prove to be an incredible source of information as her status changed to Mid-level and, at times, a High-Functioning person.

If I had a video tape rolling, this one would have been a bestseller. In fact, seriously, Mary is better than many of the actors and actresses in the movies and on television, the only one she can't fool is a Los Angeles County Judge. If I wanted to, I could not make this stuff up because Mary's actions go beyond imagination!

Listening to Mary talk is at times surreal. She has a loud and raspy voice and locals tell us that she has been on the television program

COPS more than once. One informant close to her told me she is able to survive because she receives a monthly check from Social Services, and what little she does receive, she spends buying beer or showing her generosity to others. Mary's moods change quickly. She goes from loving and sweet to physically violent and verbally aggressive with no warning.

Last year during our trip from San Francisco to Venice Beach, I purchased a pair of Nike sneakers, and since Mary was shoeless when I first met her, I gave her my newly purchased sneakers and a pair of socks because she needed them more than I did. Mary was dirty and shoeless, and her language was vulgar. It is not uncommon for Mary to urinate on herself, blow snot, spit, throw glass bottles at people, and demonstrate a number of other offensive behaviors in public places. When she reads this, I will catch hell, but every word of what I write is accurate.

As I sat on the open front porch with some of the residents of Rose Avenue a few days after meeting her, Mary approached us and asked one resident, Sheane Gregor, whom she knew, if he could give Mary a ride to the social services building. The conversation began peacefully, but within minutes, Mary began shouting profanities at the seventy-year-old retired Grumman engineer who, unfortunately, was unable to help her because his car was in the shop. She said to Sheane, "You motherfucker, all you think about is your fucking self. I need a fucking ride downtown and you are gonna come up with some bullshit story about your fucking car. I ought to kill you, bitch." Then she got a little too close for comfort, approached me, and explained she'd kill me with a knife too. I replied, "But I just gave you the shoes off of my feet, and besides, this is America, you can't kill me." She calmed down and the building's owner told her to leave the property or the police would be called. She replied, "Fuck you all, I'll be back, motherfuckers," as she walked away. That was the first time I ever met Mary.

During the time we stayed at Rose Avenue, we developed a very informative and trustworthy source, whom we will call Robbie, who has lived in Venice Beach for more than twenty years. Robbie, like many others, knows Mary, and explained to me that Mary's erratic behavior is a result of a devastating tragedy that had taken place many years ago, landing her on Venice Beach where she tries to escape the reality of her pain. Rather than judge Mary, I was determined to get to the root of her tragedy so that I could gain a clear understanding of the cause of her homelessness. It is easy to classify her as a selfish, crude, and indifferent woman. I like the scholarly approach of learning why her behaviors are negative in addition to the behavioral patterns that define her personality. Being patient paid off. I was able to build one of the most important relationships and nurture it to discover the tragic life Mary has had.

Robbie explained that Mary spends a lot of time in and out of jail. What she really needs is an alcohol rehabilitation center. For a brief time, Mary cleaned up her act and needed a place to stay, so one kind homeowner granted her residency. The Mary we met the first time we visited Venice was very different when we arrived this time. At first, she was sober and pleasant. In a two-week period from the date we arrived, though, that sober behavior changed back to the same violent and aggressive behavior.

Day after day and night after night as we sat on our bench for the homeless, Mary was within a few feet from us, screaming aloud her favorite phrase, "motherfuckers," for no apparent reason. After asking Mary what was wrong, she explained, "Everyone wants to just screw with my life."

Mary then decided to sit in front of my feet and ask me for a favor while she drank from her beer can. I thought, *"Okay—maybe!"* She then pulled out what appeared to be a stolen credit card and driver's license, and she asked me if I would call a number so that I could persuade the person whose name was on the license and credit card to come down to Venice Beach so that we could activate his card to buy beer. I said, "Sorry, but at the least, Mary, you should call this man to come pick up what doesn't belong to you." She said, "Thanks for nothing, bitch." I quickly changed the subject, handed Mary a few dollars, encouraged her to return the credit card, and walked away. Mary was obviously heavily intoxicated. She looked like she was turning green and if she had another drink I was sure that her behavior would soon land her back in the LA County Jail.

The next night, after the credit-card incident, we were sitting in our usual spot. In front of a huge audience, Mary pushed a young girl riding a bicycle who accidentally brushed against Mary, and she said, "I love fucking with teenagers." As I predicted, Mary was headed for trouble. She was so intoxicated that she then decided to curse the world and remove her pants to urinate in public. She was wearing an orange L.A. County Jail T-shirt, screaming, "You motherfuckers, I said, you fuckers." Sometimes no matter what we do to help change people, some people just cannot be reached; but in my mind, I am not giving up on Mary as easily as she gives up on life. I felt that if I took the time to know her, there was the chance that I could befriend her and I would be able to find the good in her and learn more about her life.

Watching the faces on tourists when a situation comes to life is hard not to laugh at, especially when Mary walks up to them and says, "Sir, don't you realize you aren't supposed to ride your bike on here, motherfucker?" The stunned tourist said, "Oh, I am sorry." Mary then says to him, "Go back to Germany, and follow the law, bitch." Tourists are welcome, but follow the law, because if you don't, the homeless will remind you. On Venice Beach, though, there is never a shortage of drama. Venice is the perfect place for people-watchers to be entertained day and night!

Life is so short that I am at a point in my life where, although I don't have much, my friendship is unconditional. *Now, how many people can say that they have countless homeless friends in this country?* Most would say who cares, but my spirit is what counts. The fact that I have opened the door to another side of life leaves me open for understanding, self-growth, and awareness. That is a great triumph. I feel I benefit from knowing people with the hope that they may someday feel the same way. Time is slipping away and my time is getting shorter and shorter each day so I need to pass on that sense of enlightenment.

It was getting late and we decided to head back to our apartment. From our balcony above on Rose, we could hear Mary screaming at the top of her lungs in front of the German Beer Hall below, "Fucking Nazis, you just want to rule the fucking world. They don't want the homeless living here, but they allow fucking Nazi's to live here." Minutes later, we watched the LAPD cruiser pass by, and we believe Mary was arrested and taken away for what would probably be some time. We did not see her again for the remainder of our trip and there went my opportunity to build a relationship with one of the most popular homeless people. Nevertheless, arresting Mary is not the way to solve her problems. This is just an observation, not a diagnosis, but Mary seems to need psychological help to deal with the pain of her addictions and emotional disorder. Based on the behavior we observed when we arrived, it is obvious that Mary is capable of having good days, as you will learn. At times while sober, she is able to function and talk to people without being violent. Perhaps with proper care, Mary can have many more good days.

For a short time while Mary was not homeless due to the kindness of a friend, things were fine. However, she destroyed his property and caused havoc at the site where she was staying. Unfortunately, Mary became the victim of her own actions. However, if she is truly mentally or emotionally unfit, she may not be fully responsible for such actions.

Clearly, Mary is in desperate need of professional help, and if you did not know Mary, you would want to run away from her, but in reality, one cannot help but pity her without understanding the cause of her homelessness. I am careful not to be too judgmental because I don't yet know the facts and judging without information makes me ignorant.

There are plenty of people who can relate to Mary and her addictive, destructive lifestyle. The question is how many live this homeless lifestyle for similar reasons. I wish I could take out the crystal ball to find the answer, but what I do know is that Mary's emotional grief and pain, like Pruitt's, is something she has not been able to overcome in her life.

At this time, I was learning how to be a student of communication rather than as a professor who teaches communication. Here, I was dealing with an irrational person. With Mary, I knew I would need a great deal of patience to hear her out so that I might be able to cheer for her as she fought for survival every day. I would soon learn that this journey with the people who are homeless takes better than average communication skills. It takes an unconventional communicator, insight, patience, and strong listening skills, as well as a professional understanding of the danger that lurks. In essence, these uncommon and instinctual relationship-building skills are everything I teach my students about being an effective communicator. Trust and respect is earned.

Although Mary is unpredictable and rude at times, she helped this book tremendously by introducing me to dozens of homeless people. Ironically, Mary became one of my best allies, consultants, and sources of information.

Part 2

Chapter 7: The Low-Functioning Homeless—Not in Control

Introducing Tommy C. Manson

The sweltering and record-breaking heat wave on the East Coast and throughout the country during the summers of 2006 and 2007 took its toll on many people. On Venice Beach, we enjoyed the average high temperature of seventy-five degrees with the cool Pacific winds blowing in on us at night, and we even wore sweatshirts. No air conditioner needed!

The most common misconception about people is what we call stereotyping, but I will give you the homeless person's version of his or her own stereotype. As we get to know Mary, we learn that she was arrested that night at the German Beer Hall. Mary has nicknames and stories about every homeless person we encounter, and she names this next homeless man "Tommy C. Manson" as he searches through the garbage pails on the walk, looking for anything of substance.

Mary says, "Tommy is a Charles Manson disciple" because of her perception of his appearance. Tommy has a foot-long unkempt beard. He wears four knitted wool winter hats, one on top of the other on his head in the middle of summer, a brown leather bomber jacket over a sweatshirt, and the same blue jeans every day. He even wears bowling shoes! He also carries a folded notebook in his back pocket. His face is dirty, he picks up cigarettes from the dirty ground every few steps, and he walks fast and at times does the "moonwalk," as he turns his dirty palms inward, gliding the bowling shoes along the cement as his dance-pop action imitates Michael Jackson, who invented the walk in the 1980s. Thus, this homeless man earned the nickname Tommy C., as in the infamous "Charles" Manson from Mary.

Obviously, homeless Tommy is mentally ill and not a murderer—not that we know of, anyway—but Tommy must be approximately fifty years old and appears to be in better shape than some of the muscle-heads at Muscle Beach with all the walking he does each day. We saw him miles away at the Santa Monica Pavilion, in Marina Del Rey, which is a lengthy walk from where we stay in Venice, and he can be seen walking all over Venice Beach at specific times of the day. He consistently carries a fresh coffee cup while he bends down picking up the burnt-out cigarettes butts, but we never see him eat from the garbage pail.

One beautiful afternoon I got up the nerve to approach Tommy and speak with him. I walked up to him face to face and asked, "Excuse me, would you like a few dollars?" He completely ignored me without ever answering the question. It was like talking to an invisible person. I can only guess that given his state of mind and condition, Tommy

Manson could have thought I was a weirdo and he just went on living in Tommy's world, going about his business.

After several attempts to talk to the needy Low-Functioning Tommy, I concluded that he might be mentally beyond reach, as he never acknowledged my presence. At this time, I could not obtain his real name or why he was here in Venice living homeless. The next time we would encounter Tommy, however, was an experience we shall never forget. Tommy will be back in dramatic fashion.

Chapter 8

Julie: Beaten Down By Life

Of the countless mentally ill homeless we met, Julie is one who stands out in my mind. It is intriguing to observe the verbal and non-verbal communication skills of the homeless, especially when you try to make sense of some of the gestures they use. I have classified Julie as Low-Functioning because she has little care for her physical appearance and has no observable social and communication skills. She wears pajamas, which look like they have been glued to her body for months. Julie is covered in dirt, her fingernails are filthy, she has no shoes, and her hands are soiled. She has dirty brown hair uncombed and caked to her head, and she just sits and hums to herself.

At times, she can be exasperating. Julie may be in her fifties. She sits in one spot behind our bench in an area known as "Marijuana Hill." Marijuana Hill earns its name because it seems like people gravitate to the hill to inhale weed over other places on the beach. It gives spotters the chance to see Police from a distance better than on the lower ground.

When Jane and I try to talk with Julie, she says nothing. She seems as though she is in another dimension, like the twilight zone. As we observe her, we also observe how completely helpless she is. Sitting next to her is a very young homeless man in his twenties with a scruffy beard, torn-up jeans, and a T-shirt. He just sleeps near Julie without saying a word. Then he gets up, walks away, and says, "Fuck you." We say nothing. We think he believed we were undercover police officers because many of the homeless we met thought that and told us so.

Julie sits and uses nonverbal hand gestures, motioning in the air as though she has a paintbrush in her hand painting an invisible picture. Her face is blank as though she is in a living coma, but dying. She stares straight ahead and every once in a while she smiles. We can only wonder about what is going on in her mind.

Finally, we decided to make a last attempt to again be friendly and approach Julie without scaring her. I ask, "Hi, how are you doing?" She does not answer, not even an acknowledgement that we sit a foot in front of her. "Excuse me, are you hungry or thirsty?" I ask. Julie says nothing, not even making an attempt at eye contact. As we move back to our spot, we watch Julie walk away toward the beach and disappear into the Venice Beach sunset. We never saw Julie again. Somehow, she manages to survive in this environment.

In addition to being mentally ill, Julie looked malnourished. She is thin and frail and I wondered: where does she go to get her next meal if there is no food in the garbage pails and if she does not communicate with people? Well, apparently Julie is not alone on this issue.

Not surprising, low-income households are at risk for food insecurity. Last year, the Los Angeles Emergency Food and Shelter Local Board made it possible to distribute 34 million pounds of food for the hungry in Los Angeles County claiming that one in ten people living in Los Angeles is at risk of hunger" (Los Angeles Regional Food Bank, 2008).

In 2008, officials of the United States Council of Mayors indicated in their Status Report on Homelessness in America's Cities, a twenty-five-city survey states that "As a whole, cities reported that they are not able to meet the need for providing shelter for homelessness persons. In fact, twelve cities (52 percent) reported that they turn people away some or all of the time." Also, the average length of stay for persons in emergency shelter and transitional housing decreased from 2006. Cities reported that for households with children, the average length of a stay was 5.7 months in 2007. For singles, the average length of a single stay was reported as 4.7 months. In 2006, cities reported that an average length of stay was 8 months for both populations" (U.S. Mayor Newspaper, 2008).

In June of 2006, a study published by the Los Angeles Regional Food Bank reported that "657,000 Los Angeles County residents seek emergency food assistance from food pantries, soup kitchens and shelters served by the Food Bank each year" (Los Angeles Regional Food Bank, 2006). That five-year survey gap from 2002 to 2007 projected no change from one year to the next, which means that homelessness in America is a problem that has not gone away, even with government intervention and assistance.

The information on housing in the survey for Los Angeles is that "the Housing Authority's wait list for its fully occupied housing communities grew by more than 25% and the Section 8 wait-list grew by over 2,000 families each month." The follow-up survey showed that "As of October 2004, a total of 24,981 applicant households were awaiting their first interview" (U.S. Conference of Mayors, 2004).

What I find most important about the surveys like these is that City studies have reported overcrowding as a serious problem in Los Angeles since at least the late 1970s, (Journal of American Planning Association, Winter, 1996), and no one has been able to find a solution to the problem.

One question we can draw from the survey is how many other local governments in major metropolitan cities like Los Angeles have passed the buck on to the next generation of incoming mayoral candidates of the city only to be left for the following term or next generation of incoming mayoral candidates of the city to solve the problem of homelessness and poverty?

The bottom line is that finding a solution to homelessness is not a priority, but government funding in the United States to third-world countries is. Studies and surveys are a way for the bureaucrats to show that they are involved in change, but real change has to come from the President's office and his administration to find a solution to helping

79

the homeless rather than building the global bank of third-world countries who show little return to the United States! The fact that there are more than a million homeless children in this country is alarming. This issue of No Child Left Behind in education is meaningless for a homeless child. As a nation, don't we need to change the chances of survival for these children by providing them with hope and a future? I hope that the selling of this book can play a role in that change.

Answers come from decision-makers, policy-makers, and people who can create radical change in the system. I am not suggesting that we open the taxpayers' bank to serve the homeless, but what I am suggesting is that perhaps we can create a system that has the capable homeless working for food and shelter so that they can build better habits rather than have to depend on a system, which cannot fully serve them. Many of the people I met are not afraid to work. Looking around at some of our more polluted cities, there is plenty of garbage to pickup. Pay the homeless to pick it up; they will work.

 **Chapter 9**

Yvonne: No One in the World Should Have to Live This Way

Photo: Jane A. Lackner

No one should have to live like Yvonne as she helplessly wanders about.

Positive stories about the homeless are rare, because in general, as a nation, we are conditioned to sweep problems like homelessness under the rug and the few unmanageable homeless give all homeless a negative stereotype.

Think back for a second to your childhood: didn't our parents instill trepidation or reticence in us when we saw homeless people?

Homelessness and helplessness have an effect on people from all ethnic groups. It does not discriminate, nor do the homeless, when it comes to being a tight-knit family in helping each other.

For weeks, we observed Yvonne, a Low-Functioning homeless and helpless woman in her fifties, as she walked back and forth past us while we sat on our bench. Her lace-less sneakers make a flopping sound with each step she took until she neared our bench.

Yvonne is an African-American woman covered with dirt, and the wear and tear of the beach elements is evident on her face. She is wearing a filthy pair of what were once grey pants, and a green, dirt-caked shirt. Yvonne represents the epitome of homelessness. We watch her pick up cigarettes from the ground as she talks to herself. As we study Yvonne, we also meet a woman in a wheelchair and observe the painful sight of her sharing a cigarette with an unsanitary homeless man. I ask the woman in the wheelchair, "How could you share a cigarette with someone; aren't you afraid of germs and catching diseases?" She replies, "We are all family and kind of have the same germs. After five years out here, it's like getting 'the shot' and you build up immunity to germs." I am blatantly honest with her and I say, "That is very disturbing. People could have all kinds of diseases like HIV and AIDS, and other things." Then she says, "Yes, you are right, but you're not homeless and you would not understand." Then she asks for money. Our attention turns back to Yvonne, who really needs money. I ask her if she had any family. Yvonne just ignores Jane and me and talks to herself, saying, "Motherfucker, you are all just motherfuckers." We walk up to her and made one more attempt to talk to her and ask if she is hungry, and again, she ignores us.

Yvonne is a fixture on Venice Beach. We spotted her in the same spot each evening at the exact same time, six o'clock. Sadly, she could be someone's mother or grandmother, sister or daughter. Observing Yvonne lying face down in the sand the next day is pitiful. It serves as a powerful reminder that there are people suffering every day in the world, even in America. The question remains: why doesn't she receive help? Many of the homeless need medical attention and are blatantly ignored.

We followed more people like Yvonne and observed the same patterns of mental disturbances. People with severe mental illness and substance-abuse problems should be receiving treatment, even if the police take them in to have them admitted. In my view, I feel the community should see to it that the homeless and mentally disturbed receive the treatment they deserve. To watch a person day after day in a state of absolute disarray is beyond painful. Yvonne had not bathed in weeks. People feel they can't get involved. More than five times we walked up to Yvonne and handed her food and water, and even left clothes on the bench for her and other homeless people. In fact, I arrived in California with a full suitcase, but when I left, 90 percent of the clothes I had with me I left for the homeless. Yvonne and people like her are too mentally ill to ask for help themselves; they need someone to reach out to help them. A few dollars or a couple of free meals are not going to fix Yvonne's problems.

It is clear that there are many homeless people fending for themselves on the streets of Los Angeles and around the world without intervention from the government or mental health professions.

Chapter 10

Jason: Disturbed by a Milano Cookie

Photo: Jane A. Lackner

Jason gets the rest he needs before fighting himself and "The Wall"

Another homeless person who falls under the mentally disturbed category of homeless is a man I have observed for the past three years who walks the Ocean Front Walk. Jason is a thirty-three-year-old Low-Functioning man from Maryland. As with Tommy C. Manson, I never had the nerve to approach Jason in the past because he would usually walk around on the opposite end of the beach by the Venice Pier, yelling obscenities at the breeze and talking to himself.

We stay closer to the Santa Monica Pier a few miles away, but this year, Jason parked his hotel with one bag right near our bench for the first three weeks of our final tour. This was the first time I actually was able to observe Jason up close and personal.

Jason truly wants as little contact with society and people as possible. He is over six feet tall; wears a red winter coat in the summer, tight blue—or, at times, khaki—shorts hiked up to his waist, and Nike sneakers; and has a few dreadlocks and a beard. When you look directly at Jason, he will look back, but I am not sure if he ever consciously and intentionally means to.

It took me weeks after observing Jason to actually feel comfortable enough to approach him, because next to Tommy, his behavior is one of the most unpredictable. I sat helplessly watching him day after day.

As I mentioned earlier, Mary opened the door to the "underground homeless" and people we would have never had the opportunity to communicate with. Through the transactional process of communication my relationship with Mary was beginning to grow. Watching Jason sitting against the concrete wall by our bench, I asked Mary if she knew Jason, to which she said she did. In a sober, likable state, she cordially introduced us to Jason. She said, "Jason, this is my friend Bo from New York. He is writing a book about the homeless." Jason, with his heavy red jacket, long beard that covered most of his face, and his long hair over his eyes, replied, "Oh, Hi." I was proud to have the opportunity to open a possible dialogue with Jason and finally have the chance to communicate with him.

Because Jason is antisocial, all we could gather about his trek to homelessness was that he spoke in a confused state. For example, when we asked the question of how he landed on Venice Beach, he said, "I got here by bus, dude. I screwed up a little and left home to live in California." When Jason finally calmed down after an hour, I asked him where he was from, and he told me, "Maryland." I asked him how long he had been homeless and he had no trouble being honest. He said he had been homeless three years and he liked California. Since I had observed him for three years, I knew he was telling the truth.

He said California was a place he always wanted to visit. This left him with a broken life, homeless, walking around with a blanket, eating from garbage pails, and picking up cigarettes from the ground and smoking them. Although his actions in public are hard to ignore, he remains a very private person. Since my selection of observing the homeless is a random sample, I found that some homeless shared their story more willingly than others.

Across the walk from the homeless bench I observe a few stores. When the stores close there is graffiti on the security gates with some spooky paintings of what appear to be ghosts and other painted images that seem to represent the dark side. Each night, I observed Jason stake out this graffiti until late hours of the night. Jason sits stationary, literally all day; he sits himself across from the wall and watches the store all day, cursing at it, yelling at himself, using profanities, and just standing up every so often to pull his shorts higher up to his chest. Jason has constant outbursts. The outbursts are so violent that he punches his palm with his fist as hard as he can and then he violently kicks the air or the cement wall in front of him. This goes on all day and night until he exhausts himself to sleep!

When the store rolls the metal overhead gate down at the end of the day, I believe that to Jason the wall comes alive, because he screams loudly at the faces and graffiti painted on the wall, repeating, "Fuck you, what are you looking at, bitch." This goes on for the public to view for more than forty-five minutes as we watch him punch and kick himself, while staring at the wall.

Mary, who is sitting with us, approaches Jason and says to Jason as he sits down, "Jason, honey, Bo is worried you are going to break your foot from kicking the cement." *Great, Mary,* I think, *go right ahead and tell him it is me who is worried that Jason will break his leg.* Jason responds, "Get out of the way and leave me alone, Mary."

All I can think about is the broken life Jason has, and this was a case of hopelessness because without professional intervention people like Jason face a dismal future. I am more worried that Jason may get angry enough to hit Mary. Mary reminds me that she has been raped, kicked, punched, ambushed, and cursed at for years on this beach, and she is not afraid of anyone, another reason why I am careful not to misjudge her as a selfish woman whose life is filled with poor choices. She says that Jason is just trying to work the demons out of his head, while Mary admits she is crazy, yet compared to Jason, she is higher functioning.

Finally, I go up to my apartment and get Jason three apples and a bottle of cranberry juice. I am wearing a bandana, military pants, and a T-shirt. I reintroduce myself and say, "Hey, how are you Jason?" He replies very politely, "Fine, thank you, how are you?" I am so surprised at how he can go from rage to answering me in a friendly and normal tone in two seconds. This cannot be too bad for the moment, but I am also cautious in my approach with Jason.

Understanding people like Jason helps me to make predictions about Jason's behavior, especially since I can now understand his non-verbal communication cues, which transform him in and out of his stages of anger and rage. When Jason starts to punch himself, obviously that is the cue to stay away, but then he has moments of kindness and friendliness during the day. Another habit he has is that he scratches himself so hard that it looks painful, almost as if he is trying to get out of his own skin.

Watching Jason transform in and out of character has me very interested in abnormal psychology and the need to further understand why we allow mentally ill homeless to care for themselves.

As I try to gather more information from Jason, he goes right back into his violent psychotic mode and says to himself, "Bitch, what the fuck are you looking at," as he stares at the wall, pulls his necklace up to his mouth, and kisses it. I walk away for now, but I know that there is hope to learn more by the end of the trip.

One of the things I wanted to ask Jason before I left this summer was what he saw when he closed in on that wall.

The following week I asked after some relationship-building, but Jason said, "You're asking all the wrong questions, dog." To me, this meant "None of your business." I got the memo! Understanding Jason might be beyond my realm of capability, but I made an investment in trying to understand Jason and I was sticking to it.

The next day was gorgeous, and after a great day at the beach watching the seagulls pick up toys from where children left them, we brought bread out to feed the birds, but then realized that the police would ticket us if they caught us feeding the birds.

Jane and I sat on our bench at around seven p.m. Thousands of people were strolling on the walk today, and Jason sat five feet away from us. I asked Jason if I could do anything for him, and he responded with a request for some "Top." I had no idea what Top was, but I quickly found out that it was cheap tobacco. So I walked to Henry's Market on the corner of Dudley and Speedway, and bought a box of Top and some rolling papers. I noticed that many cigarette smokers here roll their own cigarettes. Jason was happy for the cigarettes and he responded, "Thank you very much, I appreciate it."

I learned one important thing about the mentally disturbed and Low-Functioning homeless people I met: their behavioral patterns helped me to predict the best and worst times to approach and talk to them. It is so hard to watch a person who seems to have multiple personalities. One minute Jason was happy smoking, but within minutes, he went into his rage again. This time it was about something we could clearly hear. As he stared at the ground, you could barely see his eyes because his dreadlocks rolled over his face and his beard covered his mouth. Jason yelled to himself, loudly, "Bitch, why did you take the last fucking Milano [referring to a Milano cookie made by Pepperidge Farms], Goddamned bitch." He punched his fist into the palm of his hand as hard as he could. Then he screamed from across the walk at the owner of the Bistro, who couldn't hear him say, "Fuck you and your restaurant, bitch."

It was a scary thing to watch. Jason again started kicking in a jerking motion into the air, grunting very loudly, almost as if he was being struck back by another person. Now, Jane and I observed the people walking by, looking at Jason and laughing at him. Two nights later, he was gone, and we think Jason was taken into police custody in a sweep to take homeless violators sleeping on the beach. People who were now our friends told us the police did pick up a few people and some were in the exact spot that Jason stays all day. Five days later Jason reappeared.

As if the yelling that Jason did all day was not enough, later that evening at about midnight, from our apartment we could hear Jason screaming at the top of his lungs, "You fucking bitch, leave me alone, Goddamned motherfucker." This lasted for about an hour until suddenly it became peaceful, and he disappeared until the last day of our trip, when we saw him during the Hare Krishnas' Parade of the Chariots. That appeared to be too loud and too many people for Jason to handle, so he headed back to Santa Monica with a blanket over his shoulders. As the cool sixty-degree temperature at night came to an end, another person had a profound effect on me. Clearly, Jason is yet another troubling statistic and example of how the poor mental-health system here in California fails people. Jason should be receiving the proper evaluation and treatment so that his violent outburst can be controlled. With people like him out on the streets, he becomes a harm to himself and possibly others. While the system permits mentally disturbed people to roam freely about, Jason and other mentally disturbed people who are homeless transplants from other parts of the country only become a bigger part of the problem.

Helping the mentally ill is a major challenge. What is scarier than my attempts to interview the mentally ill is that apparently the mentally ill have to fend for themselves. Everyone knows who the mentally ill are, including the police, but they have their hands tied by the system.

Chapter 11

Mental Illness and the
State of Mental Hospitals

After a beautiful day on the beach, we settled into a stunning evening with the moon almost full and stars shining bright and clear. It was very quiet and I was alone, patiently waiting for familiar homeless people who might straggle by. Sitting on our bench relaxing and waiting for Jane to show up along with the regulars, I observed a homeless man I had seen many times before walk slowly up toward me. He was five feet away, but by now, I was used to living among homeless people and felt comfortable. I thought he was going to be friendly, but I was wrong. My tape recorder was rolling as I listened to the brief conversation. The homeless man resembled the rock star ZZ Top, only this guy had a bald head. He was wearing shorts and no shoes, and was carrying his life's belongings on his back. He stood still and said aloud, "The first real crime I would do was in 1980, full of money. I did six years for that. In '98 they said, why don't you sell it to the oil company, our company?" Screaming louder now, he said, "I said no, you buy the television, you take it home, you sit it down, you turn it on, you don't plug it in. You buy my light bulb, you screw it in, unplug your lamp, and [screaming] you turn it on. Calculators run off a light bulb, don't they? So will that light bulb!" Looking right at me, he yelled, "Think about it."

If you are questioning the sanity of people, you may be asking yourself, how do we as a society and the system deal with homeless people who are mentally incompetent? "Nearly a quarter of homeless have a mental illness" (National Coalition for the Homeless, 2008).

When people are mentally ill, many are admitted to nursing homes. Again, some are harmful to themselves and others. The role of people in government is supposed to be to provide programs and services for people in order to live full and productive lives. Every citizen should have that right, even the mentally disturbed. As a nation, in order to move toward positive change, we have to move beyond the shelters and implement a greater strategic plan.

In an article in *The San Francisco Nugget* titled "Ronald Reagan, The Bad and the Ugly," the article asks, "Is it any wonder that California seems to have all of the crazy homeless people? State mental hospitals were taken away by Governor Reagan in the seventies, and federal mental health programs were later taken away by President Reagan in the eighties" (Daily Nugget, June 2004).

Personally, I admired the late and former president of the United States, Ronald Reagan, but I feel he made a big mistake and did a huge disservice to the people when, as governor of California, he closed the mental health hospitals.

95

Yes, Reagan saved the taxpayers millions, but unfortunately, he left a wide-open gap in monitoring the mental stability of Low-Functioning homeless people, who could now roam freely among the general population. I have listened to and observed many of those disturbed people myself right here on Venice Beach, the very place Reagan enjoyed visiting while he was still alive.

Presidents make mistakes too!

If you are a taxpayer who does not want to pay taxes to keep the mentally disturbed in institutions, fine, but what if the mentally ill and/or disturbed person was by chance your child? We run the risk of having potentially violent and mentally ill people who cause harm to the public every day in California and around the country when there is nowhere to turn.

The National Mental Health Association reports that "Many people who are homeless and have addictive disorders want treatment, but the service system is ill-equipped to respond to their needs, leaving them with no access to treatment services and recovery supports" (Mental Health America, 2008).

Why should we care? The answer is not easy because some people bring problems upon themselves and many have hopeless futures. Others suffer from depression, and then there are those who have serious substance-abuse problems and hide life's trouble behind drugs and alcohol. Without intervention, they only become another negative statistic.

The National Mental Health Association, NMHA, reports that "Approximately 600,000 Americans who are homeless have mental illness and half of those have substance disorders." It is estimated that "90% of the homeless have prior work histories, and 15-20% work currently" (Mental Health America, 2008). What else can we do to find solutions to the problem? Many have tried.

In fact, in January of 2005, Los Angeles County and the Los Angeles Homeless Services Authority were awarded sixty million dollars for homeless services. Thankfully, the HUD grant will help sustain 175 programs and add nine new housing projects, but it is still not adequate for the more than two hundred and fifty thousand homeless in Los Angeles. Still, the homeless population continues to grow.

In their book *A Nation in Denial: The Truth about Homelessness,* social-workers-turned-consultants Alice Baum and Don Burnes claim "that the American public has been duped by advocates into a complete misunderstanding of the pathology of homelessness in our country." The vast majority of the homeless, they say, "are on the streets not because they lack housing or because they're poor; they're on the streets because they're socially dysfunctional" (Baum and Burnes, 1993).

Many of the homeless are loners, society rejects, and mentally incompetent. Then there are those who are intelligent, articulate, and caring, and are just fed up with the way bosses treat them, so they left their jobs and found Venice as a way to exercise their right to freedom by becoming homeless. Some have a peaceful philosophy toward the government, while others have a militant philosophy regarding the government and do not believe anything the government tells us. Some even think that there is a conspiracy by our government against the people, particularly homeless people, and they blame the government for everything. Then there are those who become homeless because they are sick of the way the tax system robs them, and finally there are the unstable and insecure people whose family lives were turned upside down and into a vortex of violence and abuse against them. The homeless here are like a family too. They look out for each other; most know each other, and understand who needs love, care, and protection more than others do.

Baum and Barnes estimate that "between 65% and 85% of the homeless are mentally ill, alcoholics, drug dependent or some combination of the three. Merely providing temporary shelter to individuals with such problems is a disservice to them, as well as a waste of scarce funds. In fact, only one-third of the homeless take advantage of the public benefits that are available to them." Baum and Barnes's answer: "Treatment, treatment, treatment" (Baum and Burnes, 1993).

When there is no treatment available, then what?

Life is full of lessons, just like the people whom I write about in this book. In reality, any one of us could suffer a life-altering experience or change that could lead us to become homeless. The question is how we would personally handle that transformation if it were our mother, father, sister, or brother who suddenly met the same fate.

Dr. Martin Luther King Jr. once said, "An individual has not started living until he can rise above the narrow confines of his individualistic concerns to the broader concerns of all humanity."

Part 3
The Mid-Functioning Homeless—
Fighters

Chapter 12

Leslie: The Drama Queen

In fairness to the system, treatment services could be helpful, but a person has to want the help. Take Leslie for example, who, if I were to make an educated guess, is a Mid-Functioning homeless woman in her 30s. What a sight! During the 2006 soccer World Cup, Venice Beach was hopping with people, many of them from foreign countries.

It was as gorgeous an evening as we have seen since we have been here. Leslie apparently has many evenings like the one we are going to describe. In the middle of the walk near the Bistro Restaurant off Speedway Ave, Leslie wears a T- shirt, no shoes, and extremely low-cut jeans that allow for too much flesh to show. She is so drunk she can hardly walk, and she is dancing in front of the Bistro as the live band plays inside the bar. Patrons cheer her on.

As we sit there and watch Leslie, I say to Jane, "How on earth does a young woman like Leslie end up on a place like Venice Beach doing the things she does?" We wish we had the answer, but in trying to talk to Leslie, we do not think that we can get a straight sentence from her unless she is sober, which at this point isn't going to happen. The five or six times we saw Leslie, she was drunk beyond reason each time.

As Leslie continues to dance around the patrons of the Bistro seated outdoors, she grabs the attention of a group of young men standing on the roof of the Cadillac Hotel, which overlooks the Bistro on Dudley Avenue and the Venice Beach walk from about thirty feet above the walk. Judging by their accents, the men appear to be from Europe. They begin to yell at Leslie from above, "Take it off, take it off," referring to her top.

As Leslie stumbles to the center of the avenue with hundreds of onlookers, she takes off her shirt and rubs her crotch for the men. During this time, there are men, women, and children walking past Leslie just staring at her. She then decides that she is going to lie down on the walk and entice the men.

After Leslie screams, "Fuck all of you," we look a little closer at her and notice a huge scar from the base of her stomach to just underneath her breasts. As Leslie lies on her back, now on the grass with her shirt off, the commotion grows. One of her homeless acquaintances takes out his camera and snaps a shot of her with no top, while another homeless man named Boyd sits and enjoys the circus show and freak act as he asks her out on a date. I am disgusted. Writing about this makes me realize I can't make this stuff up.

Personally, I think that encouraging an intoxicated drunk person to behave more idiotically than she already is over the line. I ask the acquaintance to help Leslie get her clothes back on, which are now coming off from her waist down, before the police end up on the scene.

The grey-bearded bandana-wearing man whom locals call "Doc" is on his bike, and after taking pictures of Leslie's breasts, he agrees and goes over to forcefully put Leslie's shirt back on. A minute later, I no longer feel obliged as a responsible ethical citizen to feel sympathetic to Leslie in her state of mind. She decides she wants her top off and removes it again.

Leslie then runs across the walk and attempts to enter the Cadillac Hotel to join the men screaming from above. Apparently, that fails and she is thrown out, because she ends up right back by our bench. About ten minutes later, after calming down, she puts her shirt on and the LAPD arrive at the scene as Leslie acts peaceful and undisturbed next to our bench.

Essentially, the police cannot do anything unless they witness an illegal act. Is Leslie a drama queen living out her dream as an actress, or is she a deeply disturbed young alcoholic with low self-esteem? I think to myself, "Another young person wastes away to the pitfall of society."

Leslie obviously knew that she had the attention of a mass audience, and she seemed happy with it. Some nights were worse than others were for Leslie. It all depended on how much alcohol she drank. Another night, we watched her take a full can of beer and pour it over her head as the beer ran down her face and all over her clothes. Then a girlfriend of hers came up to her, hugged her, and kissed her on the lips.

Leslie apparently needs serious help with her alcohol addiction, but in reality, she may choose to live this lifestyle. We call it learned helplessness. The real heartbreak of this story is that this young woman is someone's daughter.

From a parent's perspective, knowing your child has this kind of trouble must be devastating. Once culture and upbringing is embedded into a person, though, change is more difficult because we learn behaviors and sometimes our mindset can be stubborn and averse to change. Alcoholics and drug addicts oftentimes are in denial and do not feel they need to change. Rather they blame the system and others for their behaviors until that vicious cycle brings them to the reality of the physical cause and effect of alcoholism.

All I can think of is how responsibly my students act in comparison to Leslie. I realize how lucky I am to be teaching the students at Suffolk and Nassau County Community College, and consider the real-life lessons they can learn from homeless people.

While we never saw Leslie again in our follow-up trips, Mary provided us with great information regarding Leslie last night. Leslie apparently has a stable boyfriend and is very happy. I asked Mary if this meant she has been able to beat the alcohol kick she was on, and Mary said apparently so. That is terrific!

Chapter 13

Kelly: The Homeless Beach Bully

Every class has a bully; every family has a black sheep, even Venice Beach! The night is as peaceful as they come, or so we thought. It is romantic listening to the beat and feeling the ocean breeze blowing, it is nice, and the air is cool!

Across the walk in front of us at the store, Titanic, where they sell hats, there is a thirty-year-old big-mouth named Kelly.

According to one of the locals whom we know well, Kelly is a Mid-Functioning homeless man who allegedly uses Crystal Meth, a highly addictive drug that is primarily used for recreational purposes in this country.

He is the one homeless person who makes the poor choice to be a bully, and he gives all homeless people a bad label. He is also a man that thrives on being controversial and intimidating.

Apparently, Crystal Meth induces rage in people who have a low tolerance for the drug or alcohol. As we observe Kelly walking into the Titanic, we watch him become aggressive with patrons and even one of the workers whom he appears to know.

Kelly has blonde hair and blue eyes; he wears a skater hat, a white shirt, blue Hawaiian shorts, and white knee-high socks; and he has a skateboard in his hand. After mingling about, Kelly hops on his board and, without further incident, he skates away down the walk. We know he is trouble the minute we observe his erratic behavior at the Titanic. In New York, he would have big trouble!

Hours pass by and we are still on our homeless bench enjoying the nightly show when we notice a huge party taking place in front of us at the Candle Café beside the Bistro. The people in the Bistro seem very peaceful, so does the wedding-party crowd gathering at the Candle Café. They are dressed in nice clothes for the occasion. It was a nice party, that is until Kelly shows up at about nine p.m. We are usually at the bench around that time. Apparently, Kelly was invited to the wedding party. The party has many employees in attendance from Light-Blue Bikinis-Resortwear, the bathing suit store next to the Titanic.

Venice Beach is a true skater community and Kelly, like most, uses a skateboard to get around town, but that skateboard could be dangerous and easily used as a weapon to hurt someone. Many of the people invited to the party use skateboards for their transportation too.

The second we see Kelly skate down Dudley Avenue to the café by Henry's Market and Piccolo Restaurant, we feel a little apprehensive because when we watched his behavior earlier, he was unpredictable. Suddenly, as we watch, Kelly is talking to three of the wedding-party patrons, and he pushes one of them hard enough that we can hear the thump in the person's chest when Kelly's hand hits him. Kelly is also a burly explosive guy who stands over six feet and weighs over two hundred pounds, but his mouth is bigger than his heart and brain. The person he is pushing weighs about half what Kelly does. The best man in the wedding party, who works at the head shop inside Light-Blue Bikinis-Resortwear, steps in and says to Kelly, "Dude, these are friends, man, cool out." It is like a parent reprimanding a child. The friends whom Kelly got loud with leave the party. Then Kelly walks inside the café. When he returns, he has a bottle of beer in his hand. I have always felt that beer companies should use plastic to bottle their beer because when people get "beer muscles" and feel the urge to fight, they can use that bottle to cut someone.

Being a former bouncer and bodyguard myself, I was fully aware of the problems that can occur with people who cannot manage their drinking behaviors. I worked with some tough Vietnam veterans and they taught me that those who become violent must be dealt with swiftly or things can get out of control.

I do not respect people who use drinking as an excuse to beat up innocent people. As for Kelly, he would just have to learn how to be kind to the public who wanted nothing to do with him. We are not moving from our spot, which is twenty feet from the café. The restaurant host does nothing to intervene in the confrontation between the patrons and Kelly. That is the first mistake by the restaurant. We realize that many people in Venice, including the businesspeople, take the law into their own hands and would rather ignore violent people like Kelly and deal with it their own way.

We can see why people call Venice crazy. Within twenty minutes, the patron who left from the earlier confrontation with two of his friends now returns to join the wedding party. Kelly shakes hands with them, and then again gets loud; in a flash, he pushes, and this time tries to punch the person in the face. The victim then takes a skateboard from the ground and swings it as hard as he can at Kelly, striking him on the arm. Now we have an all-out brawl as the situation becomes explosive. We recognize Dean, someone we know from the area, just as Kelly punches him in the head and chest. Kelly swings at several others, connecting with them in their faces as the blows turn to pushing and shoving.

The restaurant manager does absolutely nothing about it. All of a sudden, we find Kelly pushing people he does not know as he is yelling at them in front of Jane and me. I step up from our bench, tell Jane to call the police, and then I grab his neck and shoulder to calm him down, but he runs back by the café and breaks a beer bottle and is ranting and raving like a wild man.

After we call the police, the LAPD cruiser arrives within five minutes, with lights flashing. Kelly runs up the block screaming, "You're all a bunch of pussies." As the LAPD officer passes us, I stop him to point the direction where Kelly ran. I tell the officer he might want to call reinforcements to neutralize this person. As the reinforcements arrive, the people in the wedding party continue as though nothing ever happened. It was like a scene from the Twilight Zone. I feel like Jane and I are the only ones who care about the person who just was slammed, but even he will not press charges.

As the partygoers go right back to the business of having fun, more and more police arrive in the area to search for Kelly. People are mingling about, and then the LAPD cruiser and officer we originally spoke to returns within thirty minutes with Kelly locked up in the back seat of another PD cruiser parked in front of Henry's Market and the Cadillac Hotel, off Speedway Avenue. The officer approaches us and asks for more information and whether or not we can identify the three people Kelly assaulted. Two of them sit at the café and I approach Dean, who has just been punched by Kelly. Dean says, "Where are you coming from with that cool accent, brother?"

"New York," I say. "Listen, Dean, someone should press charges on that idiot for what he did."

Dean says, "Listen, brother, I can't get involved, man, I am on probation and can't afford to get in any trouble."

I am not deterred as I explain, "Kelly assaulted you, man, and if people like Kelly can come down here and assault you and others and get away with it, what does that accomplish?"

Dean says, "I am sorry, man, I can't help. You see, rather than press charges, people out here have a way of taking care of things like this on their own."

Then another person who works at the nearby shop who is at the party says, "Kelly will get his from the locals, man. He will have his ass kicked by the end of the week."

I then try to persuade the people whom Kelly assaulted to press charges. Nothing doing! The officer, who is very appreciative and friendly, explains to us that if no one presses charges, they will have to release Kelly. I tell the officer that it is an injustice to the public to allow this man to walk free with no accountability. The system stinks!

The officer is looking for the skateboard that was used to hit Kelly because he says he does not want to be sued for taking Kelly's board. So I ask what will happen to the tough guy and the officer tells me they are going to drop him off in "Skid Row," which is apparently a tough part of LA, like East New York, a dangerous part of town.

Usually, Jane and I are like the *National Geographic* photojournalists; we don't get involved, we observe and let nature take its course. However, tonight is different. I can't believe that a man assaults three people, the victims do nothing, the owner of the establishment does nothing, and the New Yorkers are the only ones who stand up for what they believe is right by calling the police. A senseless scene with purposeless people, we accomplished nothing! I decide it will be a long time before I get involved in something like this again.

Three nights later down toward the Southern California Presbyterian Nursing Home off Speedway and Navy Street, at the entry point to Santa Monica, we notice Kelly again as he walks up to a couple and starts talking trash, obviously trying to instigate a brawl. We just walk away and say to ourselves, "that man will meet up with the wrong person someday, and the "Bully of Venice" will become bullied by the next bully."

Chapter 14

Tracy: A Woman on a Collision Course

When people use hard drugs, they can become addicted and find themselves in situations they cannot escape or change by choice, and as a result, they sometimes are sucked into a vicious cycle that they cannot break. There are always a few who have the guts to kick the habit.

One such young woman I have been observing is Mid-Functioning Tracy. Tracy is small in stature. Watching from a distance, she appears to be like any other young person enjoying her day and night at the beach. She is five feet tall; has short dark hair and an attractive face; has on a loose shirt, shorts, and boots; and packs a hard punch. Tracy is a martial artist who enjoys using the art for the wrong reasons. One thing about Tracy is that she is tough. Tough in the sense that her personality would not allow a person in very easily. Ferocious in terms of the physical damage she can cause to a person. Building trust with these homeless women is an investment, especially since many of them do not trust men. Since I had already invested in so many other homeless people, Tracy is one that I will just present through observation, because I did not approach her. She routinely uses meth and alcohol, and she shouts profanities.

Tracy is about twenty-five years old, but she acts much younger. I think that the street life and being homeless puts her on the defensive with most people. One night at around ten p.m., as I sat talking to Adriana and Brittany, two characters whom I will introduce you to at a later point in the book, I watched Tracy argue with another homeless man named Joe, who was about fifty-five years old. Apparently Joe, in usual fashion, was calling Tracy names. In a matter of one minute, Tracy got up in his face and busted Joe in the mouth with a hard left hook, which sent Joe head-first to the cement, cutting his head open. As Joe lay on the ground, a small group of four other homeless men sat and watched Tracy without getting involved. Joe then slowly got up off the ground with blood pouring down his face, and Tracy kicked him with her boots on with a high roundhouse kick to the head, which sent Joe right back to the cement, cutting him further. Now, granted, I did not personally care for Joe because he had pulled his pants down and "mooned" me the day before when he was calling Mary names, but I did not like watching the violence, nor could I do anything about it. With four homeless men standing by and no phone, I was limited and after the Kelly incident—Booyah!

As Joe lay bleeding, Tracy decided she was not finished. She laughed first and then yelled at him, "Bitch, you still want my drink?" As she yelled, she kicked him thirteen more times in the head and stomach. Finally, a man stood in and said, "Okay, peace," and the violence stopped. It took Joe ten minutes to get up and he was a mess. There was a lot of blood. The police were never called. When Joe came over to where I was standing, I asked him if I could get him some ice. He never responded and just walked away and asked another man for a cigarette so that he could do damage control. The next day I saw Joe and he had a huge scabbing abrasion on his forehead and black eyes, busted up lip, and bumps large enough that they were clearly visible on his forehead.

As if that was not enough, Tracy, who usually hangs around on the east side of the beach, was back the next night. I was sitting with Jane, when Tracy walked right up to my face as we sat on our bench, brushed her chest against mine, and said, "You see this [pointing to her bloody cut up face], I asked to be held down and have them beat the shit out of me." I said, "Okay, who held you down?" She said, "Some people from the drum circle." I asked her, "Do you want to tell me about that?" She replied, "I have been homeless and kicking fucking ass out here since I was fourteen years old, and I am going to keep fighting." She was an inch from my face looking directly into my eyes until finally I said, "Listen Tracy, have my Gatorade, you need it more than me." I expected a fist from her, but instead she walked away. I am guessing that because I shared my drink with her, I wasn't on her hit list tonight. In addition, I was thinking maybe someone told her I was writing a book and she wanted her story to be told.

Within minutes of Tracy's walking away with my Gatorade, an older African-American homeless man slowly limped his way down to where we sat when Tracy approached the man. It was after nine p.m. and there were people eating at the Candle Café. I watched Tracy walk up to the homeless man and take his military jacket right off his back for no reason. While she was taking it off, she pulled the sleeves on the jacket to the point where the man could not move his arms to defend himself. As she did this, she punched him in his head and stomach. I was getting very concerned, and I knew against my previous statement that I had to get involved, so I yelled for someone to call the police. Instead, Tracy continued to torture this man while the patrons laughed at the man. Finally, the owner of the restaurant intervened and Tracy went about her business, but she wanted that jacket. It took time to give the jacket back to the man, who at this point was screaming, "Why the fucks are you bothering a Vietnam veteran, I am going to come back here and kills you." It goes to show what people are capable of when drugs are involved. Tracy was flying on drugs. It was obvious because she was bouncing all over the place and Hyped up to fight in a Crystal Meth induced state. This drug is ruing people's lives. After talking to Mary and seeing what she goes through as a homeless woman, and then watching the opposite with Tracy who seeks the fight, I realized that women living as homeless out here have to be tough, and men show little respect for them.

117

In 1997, The National Institute on Drug Abuse conducted a study of "432 homeless youths in Los Angeles, [in which] 71% had an alcohol or drug abuse disorder or both at the time of the survey." The study also cites that of the "600 youths living on the streets, 50% of those who had tried to kill themselves said that using alcohol or drugs had led to their suicide attempt" (National Institute on Drug Abuse, May, June 1997). Alcohol and drug usage plagues the homeless.

Chapter 15

Charlie: Another Soul Wastes Away

By now readers understand that Communicating with the homeless takes courage. The next homeless encounter is with thirty-five-year-old Mid-Functioning Charlie. It was early in the morning and I had just finished my exercise run from Venice Beach to the Santa Monica pier and back. Not many people were running about at seven thirty in the morning, but this morning a scraggly-looking male with no shirt and no shoes, wearing a leather string wrapped around his waist to hold up his ripped-up, cut-off dungaree shorts, was sitting on our bench across from The Venice Bistro.

Charlie was grimy and weathered. "What's up dude?" he asked with this deep California-surfer accent. After making our routine introductions, I responded, "Not much man, how about you?" Out of nowhere Charlie then began to recite poetry, which he called rap, off the top of his head. I could not really make out what he was mumbling, but it sounded like his own language. He said to me, "You are one ugly fucker man. Where did you get that bandana of the American flag man? I wouldn't be caught dead with that fucking flag. Fuck, dude, today's my day, I am going down to Capital Records to record my poetry. Walking right through the door, sitting down, and then turn this crystallized machine up and spit it like a bitch in heat." A little agitated I replied, "Okay, but your poetry sounds nothing like rap." He said, "Ah, that's where you are wrong, dude, and who the fuck do you think you are questioning my poetry? My poetry is rad, just listen." I thought it might be a good opportunity to move on from this subject to begin a new one with Charlie. I asked Charlie where he was from and Charlie said, "What the fuck, are you a cop or something, man? You look like a cop." "No, I am simply a friendly guy interested in people" was my response. Charlie proceeded, and so did I, but with caution. He said angrily, "I got out of jail a few months ago for drugs, man, and I have been living here for three years after living in Colorado my entire life. My family got rid of me because of my drug problems and I am not even allowed to see my nieces or nephews, man, that fucking hurts," he said with a tear running down his cheek. He asked, "Do you know what it is like to feel like the world is against you?" "Sure," I said. He said, "Why are you lying bro?"

Then I told Charlie I was sorry for him, and asked if he could do things over in his life, what would he change? Charlie, who stood about six feet tall, looked me square in the eye and said, "I don't know because I am fucked for life." He had an extended stomach, he was jaundiced, and he had a scar across his abdomen that looked a little like a wound, but could have been from an earlier operation.

Charlie then started talking about his father whom he seemed proud of, but he said he also felt like he could not live up to his father's expectations, and so he rebelled into a life using dangerous drugs and alcohol, and he had frequent trouble with the law. Charlie said, "My father was an engineer for NASA during the Apollo missions. He worked on 'MEPS' [as Charlie called it: Modularized Equipment Stowage Assembly], which contained a TV camera to record the first steps on the Moon, and EASEP" (Early Apollo Science Equipment Package), which Charlie claimed his father apparently played an important role in developing. I thought Charlie was telling the truth, since I had never heard of a MEP, and since he explained what MEP was so well, he seemed believable. I looked this information up and sure enough, there is such a mechanism.

I felt Charlie was feeling pain from my blunt and honest but non-confrontational questions, but I also felt maybe because of his regrets that Charlie was a little angry about his life and the choices he has made, so I backed off. Charlie was obviously not happy about his choices, and he alluded to the fact that his family had more than likely given him more opportunities than most, but Charlie's addictions became the central force that drove his life.

Charlie was getting too close to me and within inches of my face, an inappropriate distance in space, so I decided to sit up on the concrete wall while he sat down.

Charlie then began to tell me about his life as he calmed down, realizing that I was not posing a threat to him. He then explained that he was a former heroin addict, frequent marijuana user, heavy drinker, and Crystal Meth user. As he stood up talking to me he was shaking, and he pulled out a small shiny mirror, which I thought he might use to cut me because it was sharp enough. I moved further back and said, "Charlie, what's with the mirror?" As he made a swipe with the mirror in the air from his side to his face, he held the mirror to see his crusty mouth and replied, "Fuck, I carry this mirror so that I can be sure my teeth are still in my mouth." Once again, my perception was wrong but on the side of caution he is a stranger. I thought he might try to cut me and instead Charlie was just checking his teeth.

I learned that one of the things that can happen with frequent heroin usage or other kinds of heavy drugs is that people can lose their teeth from what is called "tooting": if you smoke the drug, over time, your teeth can become rotted and discolored.

After listening carefully, I asked Charlie what the future holds for someone as young as he, and I asked him if he thought he would get his life back together. Charlie looked into my eyes and said, "Fuck, I will die here. It's too late for me to change anything."

My conversation ended with Charlie when he said, "You're not even fucking listening to what I am telling you." He began to get confrontational.

I hope that Charlie is still alive and fighting the urges and temptations of the dark side. Charlie keeps a smile that hides a tear. He rather reminded me of the direction many people might take without the right people supporting them in their lives. Love, support, encouragement, and a whole lot of help could change Charlie's life, but it will take a "Charlie Change" in his own heart, mind, and soul in his quest for survival. Honestly, he seemed like he had a death wish. Given the fact that I watch so many of my young students with problems make a positive effort and decision to succeed and change their lives, it was so sad to watch a young soul waste away.

Chapter 16

The Venice Queen: "Talk to My Agent"

On a particularly beautiful night, Jane and I decided to sit at our bench, when we observed a man five feet from us raising a fuss on the walk. He is one of the funniest homeless people you could imagine. Steve is a forty-eight-year-old Mid-Functioning homeless man from Scottsdale, Arizona. Although his comedy was unintentional, we cheered him on in spirit. Picture a 120-pound man with blue jeans, cowboy boots and hat, hair down to his shoulders, and a weather-beaten face screaming "Beverly Hills, Scottsdale, Arizona, Rodeo Drive, Hollywood, USA" at the top of his lungs for no apparent reason. While he started out leaving a positive impression few homeless leave, he quickly succumbed to the influence of alcohol by the end of the evening.

I asked Steve how he got to this point in his life and he replied, "Fucking Greyhound bus, of course." After I rephrased the question, Steve got up from another bench next to where we took refuge, and, ignoring the question, he began to dance and continue to shout the same phrases about Beverly Hills and Rodeo Drive. Again, I asked Steve, "How did you get here?" Steve replied, "Contact Michael Griffin at Capital Records in Hollywood, he's my friend and agent, he'll tell ya everythang."

After explaining that he was a dancer for Hooters nightclub, Steve sat down to smoke what he called his "ciggy" or cigarette, and he was too exhausted to talk or scream anymore.

We did a little research on the Michael Griffin whom Steve believed was his agent, and all we could come up with was a Dr. Michael D. Griffin; NASA administrator Michael F. Griffin, who was convicted of murdering Dr. David Gunn in Pensacola, Florida; and alleged anti-abortionist Michael Griffin. But no Hollywood agent named Michael Griffin.

All Steve wanted was his cigarette, a glass of beer, and to dance and sing. As for the Hooters nightclub episode, I went back to that topic and Steve proclaimed that his girlfriend was a Hooter's nightclub dancer; "Oh, she's so beautiful," he said, as he used his hands in the air to show her body curves.

Later that evening, from our balcony, we could hear the unmistakable voice of Steve screaming at the top of his lungs, "Fuck you, fuck you, assholes," at the patrons at the Waterfront Café, the same place Mary screamed "Nazi's." Minutes later, we heard the "whoop" from an approaching LAPD cruiser. We watched the cruiser pass by and within five minutes, we no longer could see or hear Steve, nor did we see or hear him again for the remainder of our stay in Venice. The next day, locals told us that Steve is a regular on Venice Beach and they call him the "Queen of Venice." Apparently he was arrested, and according to locals who were at the restaurant, Steve resisted arrest. Darn it, the man missed his calling as a natural-born comedian. Sadly, one man walked by and said to Steve, "Shut up, you homeless piece of shit." Steve never responded. In the following trips, we did not see Steve again.

While there are those who do not like the word "homeless" to be used to describe this segment of the population, homelessness is a reality for the many faces we meet on this beach. Steve's homelessness did not interfere with his dance, his words, or his actions. His spirit is alive and regardless of how he became homeless, he seems content as long as he has a drink in his hand and people around to entertain.

The disparity in wealth in Venice is mind-blowing. On one hand, you have some of the biggest and most expensive mansions that you can imagine sitting blocks away. On the other side of paradise, you have its ugly underbelly complete with all sorts of vagrants. Visitors might think that Venice Beach is the capital of arts and freaks, and while at times we would agree with that interpretation, there is something in Venice Beach for everyone, especially homeless people. They seem to migrate here.

To understand the politics involved in how the government is addressing the homeless situation, we look to "The Economic Roundtable of Los Angeles County," which carried out research from 2002 through 2004, outlining the planning and community education in support of Bring LA Home. "Bring LA Home" was convened by city and county elected officials and is supported by a blue-ribbon panel of community leaders. Their mission is to "prevent and end homelessness in Los Angeles County by creating and implementing a comprehensive, innovative, and realistic 10-year strategic plan to end homelessness" (Bring LA Home). While the results of "Bring LA Home" are not yet officially complete, the study focuses on a long-term strategy to eliminate homelessness.

The world can dish out so much pain, but I keep thinking that the world has to become a better place where we can rid ourselves of the hate and bias, and improve life for the homeless.

Part 4:
The High-Functioning
Homeless—Intellects

 **Chapter 17**

The Captain of Venice:

Deep in the Woods

Photo: William G. O'Connell
The Captain on the edge of the continent where everyone has a home.

Many important, life-changing events happened to this country in the 1960s. President John F. Kennedy and his brother Robert were assassinated; Dr. Martin Luther King Jr. was killed; we had the Civil Rights movement, the Columbia riots, the Vietnam War, and the Kent State Massacre; the Beatles came to America; and the list is endless. This era shaped people, especially the person that we met next. He has to be one of the most colorful characters on this beach. Each character has a face, a name, and a story about life and how he or she landed here on Venice. Some openly share their triumphs, tragedies and future hopes, while there are others you can walk up to and talk to, and they never speak a word.

It is eleven p.m., when we encounter Ralph, called the "Captain of Venice," by the locals because he wears a naval captain's hat with flowers and a feather wrapped around its base. He may very well be the most charismatic homeless person I have ever met. Anyone can relate to him.

Originally, I felt the Captain was a Mid-Functioning homeless man based on my first encounter, but when he was sober, my perception changed about his functioning: he had a higher-than-average IQ. I asked him where he obtained the hat and he told me, with a salute, "The United States NAVY." The Captain had been homeless for so many years that he said he lost count. He claims he is not homeless, but in truth he is absolutely homeless by design. His story was incredible as he took me through the painful mistakes he made in his life while explaining the significance of flower power and the feather in his cap. Everything he wore represented something in his life or part of history.

Perhaps the best way to understand his movement is to watch him go into a defensive mode like a karate master. The Captain wore a filthy white sweater with five safety pins pinned to the left side of his chest. I found out that each pin had significance to his life. According to the Captain, the safety pins on his chest stood for "being derelict with his duty." Other pins represented service and the pride he had for apparently training twelve-year-old girls in Cuba how to shoot a shotgun, and for knowing how to use different artillery weapons.

I asked the Captain how he ended up in Venice Beach, and he paused with tears in his eyes and said, "You want the truth? You ever hear of Vietnam?" Yes, I replied. The Captain, now crying, said that he was from Las Vegas, Nevada, but that the war in Vietnam destroyed his life. Apparently, like so many veterans from that war, he never recovered. The Captain said that trouble came to him in the 1960s when he claimed he became involved in transferring arms to the Cubans and teaching people how to shoot weapons. He also saw many of his friends die in the Vietnam War. I am not sure if he was telling the truth about all of his crazy adventures, but the Captain was adamant in reporting his experience.

A year later, we encountered the Captain. Venice has its mystique for sure.

Initially, the evening was a sad one. We thought we learned the unfortunate fate of the Captain.

It seems that the Captain had a few drinks, went to sleep, and some say he never awoke, so we thought the worst, but only because that is what we were told. I was especially sad after hearing from Mary and another homeless man, Rodney, about what a great person the Captain was. Maybe some of the Captain's earlier stories about Cuba were not far from the truth. Before Ralph reappeared, Mary said, "Bo, the Captain often talked about 'Santa Moscow,' better known as Santa Monica, and his hate for capitalism, the very capitalism that Santa Monica represents, bitch." As stealthy as the Captain was the first time we met him, he reappeared out of nowhere, ironically just hours after we listened to Rodney and Mary tell us stories about him.

Sure enough, seeing the Captain with my own two eyes made me a believer that he is in fact alive and well. Although he lost his old beige navy hat, a newer blue cap with a pink seagull feather attached temporarily replaced it. He had one pin on his chest. I did not approach him yet because, after all, I met him a year ago when he was intoxicated, so he did not really know me at all. The Captain actually looked rested: he was clean-cut, his cheeks were rosy, and his clothes were clean.

On our last trip to finish the book, I knew I needed to get the full and complete story of the Captain's life. I realize he is harmless, but the time I first interviewed him, he made me feel like I had to be on the alert because the Captain does not like strangers getting too close to him. He used nonverbal cues, which helped us to read his next gesture and move, and his hands waved back and forth in front of me as I moved close to him. The Captain's voice was loud, but clear. This man seemed at peace with himself, and his mission was to just exist and survive the day-to-day weathering of the Venice Beach sun with a nice glass of beer, but this time, he was sober.

Finding the good in people restores faith in humankind. We really have no idea what people go through in life and I felt like it would be wrong to judge him.

Just two days before it was time to pack it in and head back east, I walked up to the Captain and I asked him if I could interview him in depth, since the last time I interviewed him he appeared intoxicated. The Captain agreed and I could not wait to interview him because I knew now he was sober this time and it would be a great interview.

In trying to confirm all of the information which the Captain provided in my first encounter with him, it turns out that the Captain was in the personnel department of the army stateside and he had to transfer files when soldiers were killed back in 1965. That can have an emotional effect on a person reading the death cards of so many people.

The Captain is one of those people who view homelessness from a thought-provoking perspective, as he took me through time from the 1960s to his life today. He started at the beginning with his childhood and pointed to that time in his life when at age fourteen he left home.

His mother died and his father was a member of the U.S. Air Corps. They traveled a lot and the Captain did not care much for his stepmother.

What I thought was special about the Captain was his compassionate demeanor, the soft tone of his voice, and his honesty. I felt like the Captain, at the age of sixty-six , is a man who reflected on his past and realized where he made mistakes, but at this time in his life, he was a big enough person to realize he was not fooling anyone but himself as he gracefully explained that he lost out on everything. That is what we call wisdom, and it sometimes takes a lifetime to realize the consequences of both good and bad choices in life. I asked him again about the feather in his cap and he told me that the feather represented his freedom to live on the edge of the continent with love and peace.

To clarify his past, taking me back in time, the Captain said he joined the military after dropping out of high school in the tenth grade. Times were different in this country during the late fifties and sixties where the relative value of a dollar bought you something. Today, the dollar is declining.

The Captain said that the military and his detrimental choices only got him in trouble, and so did living in Venice Beach.

The now extremely High-Functioning Captain never blamed anyone or said anything bad about anyone. He took full responsibility for his mistakes and the people he hurt in his life, including himself. The levels of functioning that I designed for the purposes of the book are now evident.

Under the influence of alcohol, the Captain was a Mid-Functioning homeless person, but sober he was a wonderful, intelligent person to talk to, and I learned a lot about life and gained insight from a man who had been to the other end of the earth and back.

The Captain told me he had walked to San Diego and back to Venice two times. That's roughly 130 miles one way. He had also walked to the San Bernardino Mountains, over 90 miles, but fell off a small cliff, broke his hand, and received stitches on his head over the past year, all while he was drunk. That landed him in the hospital for a month. This explains why people here thought he was dead. He was such a fixture here that when he was no longer around, people assumed the worse. The police are not out searching for missing homeless people around here, I can tell you that.

The Captain took full responsibility for everything he had done in his life, including the time he spent in jail. He said in 1963 when he lived here in Venice Beach, during the nighttime the area of Ocean Front Walk and Speedway "was loaded with dudes from all over the place, man, and a lot of them came out of Long Beach" (which is a short distance from Venice Beach).

The fine Captain continued, "At that time in 1963, they could travel freely as merchant marines because as seamen they visited a lot of ports in the far east, in which they could come into Long Beach and have their big duffle bags and they would just go right off the boat, and at that time there was no checking or anything, and they'd have a whole bag full of heroin and opium, and hashish. They had all those drugs from the east and then they'd come right here to Venice and people would come from all over the area and the base and especially UCLA at the time because they had Robert De Ropp who was doing a study called 'Drugs and the Mind' and a lot of other psychologists were doing drug studies." Venice Beach was a happening place for people committed to the drug subculture here on the beach.

After doing a little research on my own in the psychological vaults, I can confirm that the Captain's knowledge regarding De Ropp and "Drugs and the Mind" is true.

The Captain moved on to the subject of the military. He said he never served in Vietnam, but the unit that he served with for thirty-four months, the Army's 8th Infantry, 4th Division, was a crack unit that could be ready to fight anywhere in the world within seventy-two hours. The Captain said he was stationed in Seattle's Puget Sound. Puget Sound is "an arm of the Pacific Ocean, connected to the rest of the Pacific by the Strait of Juan de Fuca, in the Pacific Northwest" (Wiki Answers, Answers.com, 2008).

The Captain said that too many of his friends died in Vietnam, and working in Personnel gave him access to the records of all infantrymen serving in his company because he had to transfer their papers when they were called to serve. He said, "We knew something was coming down [referring to Vietnam] after 1963 because I had access to records and after hours I was doing false IDs for guys who were only seventeen, eighteen, nineteen, and I was getting them IDs for twenty-one, photographs and everything." I asked the Captain if this is why he went AWOL after being caught and he said, "See that is where the story gets weird. I was working with a guy who was working in the medical unit and he would order pharmaceutical drugs, and when he ordered them, the orders would go through the Personnel office where I was at. He would get the drugs and then he would clear all the papers that he had and then I would go into the office at night and get the 'file thirteen' and throw them out, giving me full access to drugs."

Doing drugs usually leads down the path of self-destruction. It did for the Captain, as he eloquently tapped into the deepest and most painful roots of his life with me. He actually brought me to tears a few times due to the simple fact that I miss my own father who passed away six years ago. I love talking to mature people because it helps me to understand a transcendental time in the world.

The Captain said that he eventually got busted, served six months in the stockade, and lost his rank and security clearance after finally being discharged. As a result of leaving the army, the Captain said, he was blackballed and couldn't get a job because when he went for a job, he was required to fill out his social security number on the application, which left the employer open to tracing his past back to the discharge he received from the army. He said, "I had a garnish on my wages because I stole so much money from the military, and anyplace that I went to get a job at that time in 1964 and '65, I had to fill out forms and they wanted my military experience, and military service was a big thing at that time, so I couldn't put anything down on paper."

There went the Captain's career, and he said the only other option for him was to be a laborer and make low wages. I asked, did being a laborer mean that he would land back on Venice Beach? The Captain laughed and said, "Actually, man, the common labor got me right back into dealing drugs. I was right back into it, and I had a thing that I was dealing a lot of drugs…'peyote' mostly."

The U.S. Drug Enforcement Agency states that "From earliest recorded time, peyote has been used by natives in northern Mexico and the southwestern United States as a part of their religious rites" (dkosopedia.com).

The cactus is well known for its psychoactive alkaloids and among these is a hallucinogenic dose called 'mescaline,' which in the 1980s I remember many people in my high school taking, although I have never personally taken the drug, nor do I use drugs.

Bringing up the subject of Cuba with the Captain is funny because, as you may recall, the first time I met the Captain he told me he was involved in military arms with the Cubans, and in particular young children who he claimed he trained to use weapons. He laughed and said, "I wasn't involved with the military at that time, this was Cuban people." "The 1961 Bay of Pigs invasion?" I asked. He said, "It was after that time, but the failed attempt to overthrow Cuban dictator Fidel Castro at that time had exiles still trying to overthrow the Cuban dictator.:" Being half Cuban, I laughed and said, "My mother has been trying to do that with all of her friends in Miami since the invasion attempt failed." He looked at me and laughed.

The Captain said he went to Florida for a while and "they had people in Florida who were Cubans who were ex-military who really were involved with the military here in the US and the military was getting weapons from other countries helping them so that they couldn't be backtracked to show that the US was involved in any way." Unfortunately, the cat was out of the bag after the first failed invasion that led to the embarrassment of the Kennedy administration.

As the drums from the Venice Beach walk banged in the background, I thought to myself that the Captain is a special man, and even with all his self-proclaimed faults, that day he felt as though he redeemed himself in the eyes of the people he is exposed to every day. I am a tourist to the Captain, but clearly, I see the goodness in a man whose life has been marked by trouble, drug and alcohol abuse, and homeless more than twenty five years.

Wisdom is a beautiful thing, especially when talking to people like the Captain because he has seen a different side to life, much of which he chose, but when you listen to him love and peace is his proclamation. I asked the Captain, if he could do something over again what would it be? He said, "It wouldn't be on this continent, I'd have a boat."

That famous hippie culture of the 60s is a memory the Captain will never forget because he was front and center in it. He said, "I was with the flower children. I was one of them. The flower children were the children of the beatniks and the intellectuals who were having difficulty with the Eisenhower administration because of the military and industry, and because of the second World War was so heavily induced by influence" from people in power. Government hardliners did not like the flower children because the perception in America was that America was losing control over the classes of people and that people were rebelling as part of a greater movement and rebellion from young people. The flower children engaged in drug use, sex, and a deep hostility and rebellion against mainstream society and toward the government who conforms people.

The Captain said that the flower children were very much misunderstood. Being one of them, he said, "The flower children were not against society, not antisocial, but the thing is it brought down the heat. They were considered communist-oriented, communist-supplied, and they were seen as trying to convert the youth of the United States, so they turned into flower children and against government reforms. They let it hang out in the streets, eating flowers, kissing babies, and sure, we might take acid, but we were harmless, man." Wow!

Sounds crazy, but not as crazy as what the Captain said when I asked him the craziest thing that he ever did. He responded with a laugh, "I wouldn't say crazy; it seemed right at the time. I went out to the desert and left my car outside of Santa Fe and I drove outside of Santa Fe with my International Harvester, had all my camping equipment and everything in it, and I just walked off and left it." I asked him how he got back. He said, "I was loaded, smoking hash, had big bags of weed. I had a lot of connections." He was twenty-four years old at the time, but he hitchhiked.

This is how one homeless person views life and how poor choices can lead to a life filled with trouble. Few of the homeless we met had the insight to realize that these choices lead to a destiny that sometimes spirals out of control. The Captain regretted deeply that when he was younger he had no education or skills to obtain a well-paying job. That, coupled with the military experience, kept him on the edge his entire life. He has also hitchhiked from Florida to New York, twelve hundred miles. He said he could write a book about that.

We try to learn from our mistakes and work on correcting our wrongs as we strive to make a difference on this planet so that the legacy we leave behind becomes a positive force in people's lives. The Captain has just created his legacy in this book. He said he has what he called a "different consciousness of existence after all the years of here and there, nowhere, somewhere, or wherever." He said, "I am in the edge of the continent here." I asked him if he had a crystal ball and could look into the future, what are some of the things he would do or change. The Captain said, "The way I look at that is simple man…Hindsight is twenty/twenty vision…you can see it real clear and understand it, but looking forward to me, man, is like being in a diesel truck with no brakes going downhill on a foggy day and curvy road in the mountains." The Captain said even people in "society life" can have life pulled out right in front of them through earthquakes, tornados, bridge collapses, and other natural catastrophes. This is right on! This happened in my own life with my son's illness.

The Captain left me with three words: "peace and love." It's the only thing to strive for.

Chapter 18

Diane: Peace and Love

Photo: Jane A. Lackner

Diane stands for Peace and Love outside her trailer.

Communicating with the bohemian and homeless sub-culture of Venice Beach invites the opportunity for intellectual discovery, physical development, and social and ethical awareness. Another person who is a spiritual and intellectual homeless person is Diane, a forty something year-old, free-spirited, blonde-haired and blue-eyed woman. Diane, along with her husband Abraham, an African American man in his fifties who is homeless by design lives in their RV. Abraham, a Vietnam veteran, said, "We have lived on Venice Beach for more than twenty years." Both are also High-Functioning.

It is another beautiful evening, ten minutes before the sunset. The moon is out. The sounds from Abraham's thumping drumbeat fills the air as he bangs the African Djembe drum until the sun goes down over the Malibu Canyon each night. Religiously, every morning at about eight thirty a.m., Abraham feeds flocks of birds just to the off Marijuana Hill near Rose Avenue. He prides himself on peace and love and what he calls "the third eye," which is the sense that helps us to use logic and reason over stupidity.

Diane has to be one of the most compassionate people I have ever met. She has a zest for life, says she is not afraid to die, and she loves animals. Diane has lived in California her entire life and her mother lives in Marina del Rey, and her daughter lives in London.

It is easy to find Diane because she is always out walking dogs or caring for her crippled pet crow, "Magic." We could not figure out whom all the different dogs belonged to, but at times we saw Diane come from her RV, which is nothing like I have ever seen. It is very colorful, like something right out of a '60s movie. The back reads "Jesus was Homeless," "I am Love," "The Spirit of Venice" and "Diane's Ark" on the back of the vehicle, which must be over twenty years old.

Other signs read: "The Bush Regime are War Criminals," and "Bring the GIs Home."

Diane is careful with people. She explained that if the police find her with her crow, it could be taken away from her and destroyed because it is not legal to have a wild animal for a pet in California. Diane has become an expert at being resourceful. I watched her sift through garbage containers finding anything from window blinds to the beautiful dress she wears while sitting on the beach. She really is an awesome person! In talking to Diane, I told her that she seems free-spirited and asked, "Where do we go to feel free?" Diane said with a smile on her face that she experiences spirituality and freedom every day. She said, "Right on, man, if you want to be free, all you have to do is say so." That is good enough for her.

After building a relationship with Diane and Abraham, we got to know their inner qualities. By our third trip to Venice, Diane owned two pigeons, and two dogs. One of the birds, a pigeon named "Holy," died the day after we were introduced to the bird, and Diane was devastated. She is a woman who loves all living things.

I asked Diane why the Police keep arresting the homeless sleeping on the beach and she said, "It used to be that poor people could live here, but now, it's unaffordable and this place [Venice] is built upon poor people. They are trying to chase them away, the poor, and make this a privatized beach. Everybody has a right to sleep. Sometimes people have no choice in the matter, they have to sleep. My friend [who was arrested for sleeping on the beach] is young, she is talented, and we should be bringing her up, not putting her in jail. It is a sin. We are not like the birds who can sleep in the trees. If you don't have a place, you have to sleep outside." Abraham said, "The police arrested more than twenty people this morning for sleeping on the beach. Possibly five women, Vietnam vets, Korean vets, people that were sick, and they let one go because they were sick. A pregnant woman was also a veteran. They [LAPD] let her go too, but said, the next time they catch her sleeping they are going to arrest her. Today is Saturday, the day after the abuse of First Amendment of people's rights to sleep on the earth. They came and took a lot of artists work, personally my art, signs that I have written about Senator McCain, Jesus, and other things that are telling people to stop killing each other."

So rather than allow Abraham his constitutional right to be vocal non-verbally, tax payer dollars are spent holding back peaceful people like Abraham.

On the war in Iraq, Abraham said, "I just don't like the idea of my brothers and sisters being killed, and that's all I have to say about that." Diane said, "There are a lot of mentally ill out here because sometimes they have been in wars that this country has created." Now they are homeless. Diane's point is, they have been abandoned and criminalized by American culture.

Every weekend Abraham plays in a band here on the beach.

That peaceful sound that Abraham creates is a reflection of the love he shows the world. These are people who care about what happens to their land, and the land that is owned by the higher power.

In talking to Diane, I had mentioned that for each book I sold I would donate a portion to the Leukemia Society and to a childhood homeless charity for educational materials for homeless children. The next day Diane approached me and said, "I was talking to the other homeless people here and they all agree that the Leukemia Society should receive the donation because those children have a greater need than us." One Love! Graciousness prevails!

Chapter 19

Life

MICHAEL

It is after nine p.m. and we are back to our bench for the homeless, where we meet and greet a truly exceptional human being. There is always a different homeless person to meet in Venice Beach. When one disappears, another appears. One person we had the opportunity to meet who chooses to live this carefree, free-expression, and homeless-by-design lifestyle is Michael.

Michael is a High-Functioning, clean-cut twenty-three-year-old. He is also a talented songwriter and a loving, aspiring musician from Philadelphia, Pennsylvania. Michael has been on Venice Beach for a few years, living the bohemian lifestyle of come and go. He has a Beach Boys sound and Carl Wilson-type voice. He hits beautiful high melodies and plays his music with a reggae symphony as he expresses himself through his music.

Michael says he does not consider himself homeless because he lives in his van.

Michael works a few days per week moving furniture and says he comes from a loving family. He usually wears the same shirt and shorts and plays in the Pacific Ocean, while strumming his guitar on the Venice Beach walk two nights a week as he moves about freely and enjoys life.

Regarding the government and education, Michael tells us in a very pleasant tone, "I have no time for college. I feel the government and college only holds people back from their freedom, and schools are just cookie cutters." He said he is content with being in the Venice Beach environment because he practices his right to be free, a common theme throughout the Venice atmosphere.

As the night moves on, I talk with Michael, and we see the strobe light of the loud and proud LAPD Helicopter scour the beach at a low altitude after nine p.m. Michael says he thinks the Los Angeles Police Department is on a mission to ruin the lives of the homeless people and the vendors on the beach.

We stand by Marijuana Hill, nearby where Coby McBee was murdered. Michael becomes very vocal about the government and police tactics. He says, "I feel it is a violation of my right to freedom to run spotlights on the beach every night. The government is becoming more of a dictatorship." Michael is totally against the war in Iraq. Michael never uses profanity, and after I interviewed him and saw him a dozen times on the walk, Michael became my friend. We are guided by love, so supporting Michael by tossing a few dollars into his open guitar case while he sings is a pleasure. He is honest, caring, and has a lot of love and peace in his heart.

Michael's personality reminded me of one of my most impressive and hardest-working students, David Lombardi, a Suffolk County Community College honors student in his last semester. On the other end of the spectrum, I shared Michael's comments with David, who is close in age, twenty-nine, and David said, "The speech you and Michael exchanged really made me think about so much stuff that not only did I but most of us take for granted...How do we define peace? How do we describe sanctuary?" David said, "Michael had a good point as well. Colleges are cookie cutters, if you really think about it. The sad truth is we go to college to not only become enlightened, but to become what the real world wants us to be and how do we really define freedom? Do we own our possessions or do they own us?"

This comes down to rules and norms in society and the issue of conformity. We all have a choice to be who we want to be in the United States. Those who wish to conform reap the rewards of what society expects us to be, sometimes without being fully satisfied. That is the point. Self-satisfaction, positive self-transformation a nd wisdom keep people in their own sanctuary of peace because they live life the way they choose to. This is the case with Michael. The one beautiful thing that education does, which I hope becomes a positive cookie cutter, is that it allows a person to remain open-minded to new ideas, opinions, and viewpoints.

Insight from people who are detached from the actual situation is a wonderful thing, as David, who lost his vision due to diabetes at the age of twenty-three, continued, "I was always told that when we look back on life, we should be proud of all of it. I look back and realize that for twenty-three years of my life all I did was take, take, take, take, and take some more. I only cared about myself and my agenda. Now all I want to do is give, give, and give back until I am blue in the face. There are many good people living on the streets and for those who are homeless by design, I give them so much love because they are living in every sense of the word free."

I believe David and Michael would be good friends if they ever met. Education is a powerful tool for self-empowerment. It helps us to understand why the world is the way it is and why we take different paths in life as we wonder about trying to find ourselves.

Chapter 20

Jessie: "What Is Anyone's Purpose?"

Jane and I strolled onto the beach at around ten p.m., and we could just about make out what appeared to be a man wearing a light-colored trench coat. Minutes later, as we began to walk through the sand to talk to the shadow, we could hear him vomiting profusely. Apparently, he was eating what must have been old and rotten food from a garbage pail.

After we realized he was okay, we approached him with a bag of cookies which we decided we'd had enough of; so as Jessie, a twenty-four-year-old man from Chicago, came face to face with us, we handed him the cookies, and I asked him, "What's up, man?" I told him my name and said, "If you don't mind me asking, how did you become homeless?" Jessie stood over six feet and he had long, greasy, dirty blonde hair with a very handsome face and slight goatee. He was wearing what was once a light-colored pair of jeans, which were now aged and filthy. Jessie replied, "Shit, how does anyone get the way they are? How did you get to be the way you are?" Good answer! Jessie had me thinking.

What makes a person with his drive suddenly take a twist? Then Jessie, who at first was apprehensive, finally became a little more comfortable since I was not posing a threat. He explained that he had been living in Venice for two years after leaving his hometown in Chicago, and he became deeply involved in drug usage, but managed to complete his degree in business from the University of Illinois.

Jessie said, "I am at peace here, man. What else could I possibly need, this is the free zone. I love nature, the ocean, and the stars and moon....I am at peace." I looked at Jessie and responded, "But you could really make something of yourself at your age," and Jessie replied, "When I get my life together, maybe I will."

As a communicator, Jessie was articulate and a bit more High-Functioning than some of the homeless we met, yet he was still reliant on a garbage pail for food. His mid-western dialect and perfect pronunciation of English—American Standard as we call it on the speech and debate circuit—was effective.

Jessie said he was very confident in his ability to find his next meal, but also explained that sometimes it hurt to eat from the garbage pails of Venice in order to survive. He was also thankful for any gift of kindness from a total stranger. Before walking away, I asked Jessie, "Don't you have a purpose?" Jessie replied with a question, "What is any of our purpose? Do you have a purpose?" I said, "You want me to answer that?" "Yes," he replied. I said, "My purpose is to try to find peace on earth just like you, but in my life the true purpose is to make a difference in the lives of others." Jessie looked at me with a smile and said, "That was really nice, thank you."

As a parent, all I could think about was that Jessie was someone's son. I would be devastated if my Colin was homeless. Jessie truly had potential to make positive changes in his life, especially at his young age. I wished we could further help him with some kind of "Homeless Intervention Program" whereby trained educators or professionals could step up and reinforce the benefit of education so that people with the potential similar to Jessie's could find a way to contribute in a positive way to society. Again, drug usage is the pitfall of American culture.

Part 5
The Return

Chapter 21

The Venice Beach Counterculture
A Year Later

June 30, 2007

It has been more than two summers of observing the homeless in Venice Beach from the idea phase to the research and trust-building phase. Finally, my best teammate Jane and I are back in Venice to complete the book. In that time, I have come to the realization that there are two philosophies that exist amongst many of the homeless here. First, there are those who conform, and then we have the nonconformists who rebel against a system; its curriculum; and the rules, norms, and standards we are normally accustomed to as law abiding people.

I waste no time and head toward our homeless bench, and sitting on it is a homeless woman with a cast on her leg. I ask the woman if she would like to be in my book about homelessness. She answers, "Fuck you, and you better not take a fucking photo of me, bitch." The word of the day and every day after is "fuck," and "bitch," two favorites used by most of the cohorts here. It's just words. *Ah, Venice*

Beach, California! I thought, it's not for everyone, but if you like entertainment, it is here my brothers and sisters.

In New York, people have set expectations of the glamorous big-city life. Venice Beach is similar to Greenwich Village in New York City—the theme of the regulars is that they are people who are free to be who they want without a curriculum or cultural code of norms and rules where nonconformists, intellects, buskers, bohemians, and dog walkers can claim the territory "the free zone."

Venice Beach provides the only free zones, where people can go about their day in a roseate way without people ridiculing them. When you visit these places, it is important to go with an open mind.

In Venice Beach, some things never change and then others have. Dick Neal, owner of the apartment we used to rent on Rose Avenue, has died. He was a wonderful man. As a result, we now rent two blocks away at an even nicer place on Dudley at the incredible Venice Suites.

I ask Jane to get more involved in writing the book by taking photos. She is a terrific photographer. She agrees to help me to finish the book, but not without risks.

Chapter 22

The Wind Cries Mary

Photo: Jane A. Lackner

Homeless more than 20 years, Crazy Mary, arrested more than 180 times by LAPD tells O'Connell the tragic circumstances of her life.

As fate would have it, the intrigue and magic of Venice are nothing short of spectacular.

Walking toward Henry's Market off Dudley and Speedway, I run into Crazy Mary. In Mary, there is as much to love and pity as there is to laugh at. She has endurance and though her foolishness makes her unwittingly cruel at times, there is tenderness in her personality when she is free from intoxication. Many people completely misunderstand and have little patience for Mary, including me at times, but as I promised, I will succeed in getting to know her. When Mary showed true signs of remembering me from year to year, our acquaintance developed into a meaningful friendship that is hard to describe. I also thought about my role in education as a professor, and realized that my taking the time to understand Mary's life would help to enlighten my students and provide the opportunity to teach people about a social problem that plagues the world, not just the United States. From the moment I met her, Mary intrigued me because of her toughness to survive in this environment.

On this day, a year after I saw her last, Mary is dressed like the late singer Janice Joplin. She has on purple sunglasses; she is wearing a historical hat like the one Superman wore, and a skirt. I even saw her on a piece called "Beach Bum Boxing, Venice Beach, Crazy Mary" on YouTube where you can see how people use Mary to enhance their comedic videos as they exploit her and use her for their comic relief.

Mary said, "I just got out of the penitentiary and they told me I need to get a psychological evaluation. I spent nine months with eighteen hundred women." Why? I asked. She alleged, "That man who sleeps over there, Sammy, a Vietnam veteran [pointing to the spot], took my shit and threatened me. I got a hold of a big ol' steak knife and was gonna stab him because he was going to rape me and beat me up." One of my other homeless friends actually said Sammy tried to rape her as well.

In this case, when Mary went on the attack to apparently defend herself, the police arrested her. With her record, I honestly feel that she has become an easy target for police regardless of who is at fault. I told her that it was a good idea to get a psychological evaluation so that she could get the help she needed. I also mentioned to her that last year just before her arrest, I felt she was heading downhill. In a drunken state, she said, "Bullshit." I reminded her that she stripped down out of her clothes in front of a large crowd on the walk. "Listen, motherfucker," she said, "Do you want to fuck me?" *Oh, lord!* I thought. Well, after I listened to Mary tell me about what she had done in the past year, she said, "Well, since you don't want to fuck me, I need to go watch the JFK conspiracy. Do you know that there was a conspiracy to kill our president?" she said. "Fuck it, you don't know shit," she said.

One of the things I regret about Mary was that she yelled at me the very first time I met her. I knew that sometimes a person just needs someone to talk to and I felt that I failed in communicating with her. After all, we really did not know each other, but had I taken a more understanding approach the last time, Mary might have seen me as a friend instead of a person who found fault with everything she did, so this time around I was determined to learn from her. I am glad I was patient because it paid off.

As unpredictable as the Mid-Functioning Mary's behavior can be to us, she showed her lovable side on this trip on every level. Mary finally found someone who would listen to her. She told us she has been raped countless times, and about her involvement in two difficult situations: a robbery her friends committed, and the alleged killing of one of her friends by the DEA in Austin, Texas during her drug days. Both became pivotal downfalls in her life. One person she knew robbed a liquor store on Navy Street, which was a block away from where we were standing, and the story was not clear as to her role in the robbery, but the friend was caught and imprisoned for a consider-able amount of time.

The friend in Austin, Texas who was killed was killed in a raid by the DEA, she said. Mary said, "We had no drugs on us, but the Agents stormed the house, and thought she [her friend] was reaching for a gun, and [now crying] shot her. Man, it was fucked up, the babies were eating shit from their own diapers, there were rats all over the house, roaches everywhere, fuck, and it was a horror scene. The kids lost their mother, the babies were taken away, and my friend wasn't the one with the drugs, it was her husband." I did my best to get more on this subject from Mary, but she said she didn't want to talk about it again.

Another completely tragic incident involved Mary's brother who left her with his child. Mary left the child for a few minutes by a body of water only to return to a drowning child. The child died. This hor-rific tragedy was one that left me speechless. It helps to peer into the main causes behind Mary's self-image and how she views others. She views herself as worthless and as someone who has made irreversible mistakes that can never be corrected. That is why it is easier to live life on the bottle. It hides the pain and helps her to dismiss her guilty conscience while the better side of her shows what little love she may have left, but is afraid to show it.

Reality is a powerful leveling force for most of us, and then for others like Mary, the system tries to keep her held down without any psychological investment in correcting her behaviors. As I look down Mary's rap sheet, which is sixteen pages long, I find she has been arrested for disturbing the peace, battery, assault with a deadly weapon, disorderly conduct, prostitution, battery against a peace officer several times, vandalism, indecent exposure, threatening a crime with the intent to terrorize, resisting a public officer, soliciting a lewd act, and petty theft. Mary was convicted of selling marijuana and hash to a police officer, which she did three hundred days in jail for, contempt of court, reporting a false emergency, challenging to fight a person in a public place, disobeying a court order, and public intoxication. Her fingerprints led back to her using more than twenty-five aliases.

On the other side of Mary's explosive and self-destructive behavior, she has a caring, sensitive side to her. To really know Mary is to love her. Her pain is so deep that I had trouble making sense of why people turn their lives into a tornado of devastation and a life of emotional suffering. Mary has never recovered from things that take time to heal. She has seen or been part of things that we read about in the papers or see on the big screen.

Given her mental state, which at times is excellent, Mary has an opportunity to let the system help her. Each time she does, she unfortunately turns right back to the drink. It is her downfall. One day she would be our best friend, and as soon as she began drinking, the alcohol took over and the lovable Mary disappeared. Personally, I have never been drunk in my life and I hate alcohol because I see the devastation it causes!

After consistently seeing Mary over the next few nights and up until the time we completed our trip, this time we really got the opportunity to get to know her struggles, her battles with the police and the other homeless, and the inner turmoil that eats at her soul every day. I also knew that getting to know Mary would take my best communication skills because I knew that if I said one wrong thing, she might abandon our newly formed relationship. I begin slowly and the trust grew into a bond and she agreed to let me peer into the most painful moments in her life as she explained throughout the rest of our time together her reasons for living in pain with constant reminders of her beautiful son, Sean.

I also felt it was important to get accurate information firsthand from her, because some of the things people told me about her last year I felt might not have been true. She asked if I could buy her a pack of cigarettes and we started talking.

As Jane walked about taking photos, Mary and I had a real heart-to-heart discussion. She began by telling me about her seven-year-old son, Sean, who she said was institutionalized as a child, and was taken away from Mary when she was much younger because she was a drug user and an alcoholic. She blames herself for the unfortunate circumstances her son had to endure. Mary said that she did the best she could with what she had and although it was not much, she loved her child. Like many Americans, Mary is faced with addictions. The addictions coupled with having a child with a disability made Mary feel like she failed both her son and in life. According to Mary, "Sean was born deaf, but I loved him so much more than I love myself." As her eyes welled with tears, Mary said that at age twelve, Sean escaped from the institution where he had been placed and he apparently stole a van to get away. It was a cold icy day in January when Mary received the horrific news that her son had sideswiped a car and run into another car while the police in Chicago were chasing him. The crash killed her son instantly. Imagine not having a photo of your own child. Mary's life has been so torn, she has few valuables on her person. It seems as though some people are just cursed from birth.

The attitude of many of the homeless we met was one filled with a sense of loss of self. Mary said, "I drink to wash away the pain, do you understand, Bo?" I cried with Mary because I could sympathize and feel the pain of her deep tragedy. Later that same night after talking to Mary, I gave her my sweatpants and a brand-new shirt because she was cold. All she owned was a sleeping bag, a small bag of clothes, the clothes she had on, and another small bag filled with twenty golf balls. She did not wear a knapsack because she said she was afraid that if she was ambushed, the attackers may pull her to the ground by the knapsack and beat her senseless. It is not uncommon for homeless people to be robbed of what little valuables they have, and beaten by other homeless people.

Weeks later as I walked the Ocean Front Walk with Mary to take her photo for the book, I walked into a few good men whose opinions on homelessness and Venice Beach I wanted to ask. Mary stopped to talk to people she knew, as she knows nearly all the vendors, while I interviewed a life-loving, intelligent African-American man named Reggie, a cross-country truck driver from Utah.

Reggie said that the homeless in Venice survive here because they do not have to deal with the elements of the weather in the wintertime like the homeless in Utah. In Utah, Reggie said that there are facilities set up that engage the homeless population in order to try to help the homeless get back on their feet to live productive lives. Reggie and I talked about the aftermath of September 11 and the tough streets of New York, and about music and how it has influenced our young people. He said that he is "old school" and his musical influences were groups like the Temptations, the Beatles, and musical genius Stevie Wonder. He said that rap music is full of negative messages and our children have lost the dimension of respect that he said he had growing up.

Reggie said today, more than ever before, people use knives and guns to solve problems and people have trouble solving their differences by talking things out. "We don't communicate anymore," said Reggie.

Speaking of communication and conflict, as Reggie was telling me his interesting and sensible philosophy on life, a self-proclaimed Rasta man came up to Mary and he screamed at Mary because she asked him if he got his leather jacket from the garbage pail. He said, "Listen, you bitch, if you touch me, I will kill you. Just try me. I am a Rasta warrior, and just try to touch me, you bitch, I'll guarantee, I'll fucking kill you." He was about six feet four and very angry. This is not the typical Rastafarian philosophy, I thought. Rastas are about clearing up misconceptions, peace, and rebellion for the betterment of humankind, not the violent destruction of people.

As the Rasta man walked away, Reggie and his three friends just looked at me and said, "Man, that guy is out of his mind and he is lucky he did not touch that woman," referring to Mary of all people.

Mary then started to tell me this story about how while she was in prison she thought about this "contract out on [her] life," and upon her return from the "big house," she walked in on what she called her "celebration wake" on the beach where she claims other homeless people were "celebrating [her] death." She had a fit and began yelling at the circle of homeless people, who must have been joking about her being dead. Obviously there was no contract out on her life, I told her. There was no reason for it. Mary said that the conspiracy involved several people. She oftentimes introduced me to people as her son, specifically one man who was a street performer whom she hated. If you visit Venice Beach, you can't miss the man. He is a dark-skinned man who wears an American flag bikini and bright contact lenses, and he uses a heavy metal ball, the size of a baseball, which he performs tricks with as the ball rolls up and down his arms.

Mary walked right up to the man and told her I was going to "kick the shit out of him," and that I was her bodyguard. I thought to myself, *this woman is going to get me in a fight or killed by the end of this trip.* The price we pay for an interview. The man apparently used Mace on Mary just before she went back to jail because she was drunk and got too close to him.

Mace on Mary?

Couldn't he use common sense and walk away? The worst part is that as Mary and I walked, there was an LAPD cruiser stopped and the officers were out of their car. Mary walked right up to them and started talking. She introduced me to them as Bo from New York, and told them that I was writing a book on homelessness. The officer was very friendly and Mary then told the officer, "You know that little mother-fucker sprayed me with Mace and he got away with it? They stole my blankets and everything." The officer said to Mary, "Sometimes you can be aggressive, Mary. Remember that time I 'tasered' you when you became violent?" Mary argued with the officer that he didn't use a stun gun to arrest her and she began to walk away. I asked the officer if it is legal to walk around Macing people because I did not think it was right for a man to Mace a homeless woman in the face. The officer told me it is legal if the man felt threatened and that in the case of Mary, she can become violent and hurt herself or someone else. As we walked away, Mary was crying and she said to the officer, "Fucking Nazis." For me, I was again left speechless and just stuck in the moment. By now, there really is not much a person can throw at me that I have not heard or seen. This whole experience was life altering.

The truth is Mary is her own worst enemy. It is so heart-wrenching to watch a person self-destruct. Now that she is out on parole for twenty-four months, which could change any day, she drinks and prostitutes herself to different people in the neighborhood she knows, including one store owner whom we observed asking Mary for a favor. He paid her $4 for sex. That is how desperate people can become to eat, drink alcohol, and survive. In order for Mary to get the proper services from Social Security, Mary would need a sponsor who could be her guardian in a sense, but nobody here will do that for her because of her record of accomplishment and pattern of turning on people. That married store owner recently had a massive heart attack and is now dead, while Mary heads back to prison not knowing about the death of the store owner who paid the four dollar trick for Mary's prostitution.

Mary is proud to use obscenities because, according to Mary, this is her way of surviving. The only person she says was supportive of her was the Captain. Mary said that the Captain taught her how to survive. I said, "You mean he taught you to be a prostitute?" "No, bitch, that is not what I meant, he taught me how to fight these fuckers off who are trying to kill me on this beach," she said.

Chapter 23

The Underground Homeless

It is funny how fate works. Mary, a person who I never thought could be friendly with me, now got me a free pass into the "homeless underground" as she introduced me to a handful of other homeless people I wanted to meet, but would have never been able to meet. I was very curious to meet and learn about them, but I was also cautious with some of them. Although she did not like him, one man Mary introduced us to was, Eric. He stumbled up to us swaying back and forth in a semi-drunken state. Eric was over six feet tall. He was wearing red shorts, was covered with tattoos, was bisexual according to Mary, and he had on a blue jacket. Mary didn't like Eric and she made it clear by telling him to back off, but he continued to stay close. He was getting a little too close to me, and was now invading my personal space. While he was swaying back and forth, I handed my camera, glasses, and bag to Jane, and I was ready to get a little defensive if I had to. I said to Eric, who inched his way closer to my personal space, "Okay, that is close enough, step away from me." He stood right back and said, "Man, I am not going to touch anyone." In retrospect, he was so intoxicated I don't think he could harm a fly as he turned out to be harmless. But, I told him, "No, really you are not going to touch anyone. Don't do something you might regret." I meant it. I had to protect Jane at all costs.

Mary was too funny. She claimed that Eric, a Caucasian male, was from the gang the "Bloods." I laughed and informed Mary that she might have bad information here. From everything I understand about the Bloods and gangs, they do not allow Caucasian males like Eric into their gang, especially one who spills his guts when you ask a question. The problem was Eric was incomprehensible as he mumbled his words. This tells me that Mary's perception of others is also based on her own experiences with people and her stereotypes and typecasts.

Mark, Kim, and Patty

The night was a perfect Venice night, seventy degrees, a cool breeze blowing in from the Pacific Ocean, and we were standing in a small circle by Marijuana Hill. Jane, my new homeless acquaintance Mark, Mary, myself, and a man with "exceptionalities" (as my students would term it) by the name of Kim, who was sitting in a wheel chair, with no legs, were all relaxed and talking. For a second I thought to myself, what am I doing here? This was a very odd mix of people, but somehow with all my street smarts, I felt that Jane and I could fit in. I asked Jane what she felt about helping me with this project. Jane said, "It is an eye-opening experience that has taught me not to stereotype the homeless."

175

People ask me if I was afraid during the experience, and I say, sometimes. I keep in mind that they are people like us, just with addictions, mental illness and other problems. To me, the fact is that people I know in my own life have similar problems, but are just not homeless. People are people, whatever their situation may be, so sometimes I was scared and sometimes not. They are not animals.

Since these people are new to the book, I will tell a little about each of them with the same humble enthusiasm.

Down the bike path overlooking the beach rode Patty on her bicycle. She stopped to say hi to Mary. Patty, a High-Functioning homeless woman, has been homeless for thirty years by choice.

Of all the homeless people I met, Patty, and the 'Chief' who you will meet shortly, are two of the highest-functioning. They are an absolute pleasure to talk with. They seem to fit their constitution into the confines of the Venice Beach carefree attitude.

Patty began telling me that the reason she was homeless was that thirty years ago she was evicted from her apartment. She said, "Why pay rent to a landlord who just capitalizes on your money when I can live free?" She decided to live in her van, a 1973 Dodge. To this day, she still lives in the same Dodge van on church property in Santa Monica. She said, "I am happy, I pay no rent, I work, I live on the church grounds, and I live what I call a good life. I eat nutritious food not out of garbage pails, and I am not harassed by the police because I know better than to stay in one place and be labeled by the police as a homeless pitiful woman. I take care of myself. I have clean clothes, I take showers, and I am responsible for myself."

Patty is as free as a homeless person can be. She explained to me that being a vehicular homeless person means that she still lives the homeless lifestyle, but she sleeps in her van, has a bike, and she doesn't use drugs or drink. She is one of the few who have their lives in order. She will not be rich and famous, nor does she care to be, but she has what many do not: happiness.

Then we met the complete opposite of Patty, as I went from a woman who has it together to a man who is troubled by life. Mark was another one of Mary's temporary transient homeless acquaintances who was not necessarily her friend, but he spent a short time trying to befriend her.

Mark's red shirt read "G_ F_ _k Y_urs_lf" across the front. Mark is a Mid-Functioning homeless man in his thirties and over six feet tall. He told me he had been in and out of prison, but never got into detail about how he landed in prison or how he became homeless. When it comes to prison life, it is easy to assume that if a person is in and out of prison, he or she is troubled. Mark did tell me a story about when he was younger. He said that when he was nineteen, he went to kill a man who raped his friend's daughter, but the police had captured the rapist before Mark and his friend could kill him. Mark said, "My friend called me and said, 'Man, I need your help to kill the guy who raped my daughter.'" Mark said he felt it was the right thing to do to go kill this person. With this kind of mentality, I knew that I would run into some potentially dangerous homeless people and I would have to develop a deeper awareness of the dangers of dealing with strangers. If someone could have that attitude about murder, I wasn't about to be on the LA statistic list for another one.

Mark was saying that dealing with the LAPD requires a person to adjust his or her attitude. He said Mary has the "no-care" attitude toward the LAPD because she has been arrested almost two hundred times, but for Mark, he said, "You just have to know your space and when to stay of the way of the LAPD and not look for trouble."

Mary later disowned Mark after he urinated in front of her on her way back from the Social Security building where she picks up her monthly check. She said that Mark crossed the line of respect and that disrespecting her means he lost a friend in Mary. Even for Mary there is a level and standard that she defines as unacceptable behavior.

Chapter 24

Homeless Women and Children and Abuse

The beach attracts all kinds. One late afternoon, a woman and some of her friends, some of whom were homeless, were sitting behind our bench. The woman let her daughter roam around while she looked after the child from a short distance. The child was approximately six years old. While the mother took a few hits from her friend's marijuana pipe, the child was running and fell on the cement walk. She was bleeding and crying, and her knees were scraped from the fall. A man went over and brought the child back to the mother and rather than comforting the child, the mother began yelling at the child and hit her. It was very disturbing. The mother allows her daughter to be exposed to drugs and lacks childcare, and the child becomes another victim of her mother's circumstances.

On the other side of the coin, you have other homeless women we met who said they are called names, beaten, used, raped, and involved in a cycle of violence that is hard to put into perspective. Some will also do whatever it takes to support their drug or alcohol addiction.

There are too many deadbeat fathers in this country and the system has to crack down to enforce the laws of each state. One homeless person we met, Alex, told us that instead of paying child support and alimony, he became homeless, another new twist on homelessness. Now he lives this homeless life and is invisible to the system because no one can track him down on the radar. The man is young and capable enough to hold a job but too selfish to want to support the children he helped bring into this world.

The National Coalition for the Homeless (NCH) states, "One of the fastest growing statistical segments of the U.S. homeless population is single women with children. Lack of affordable healthcare, coupled with a catastrophic family illness, is a growing reason why many formerly working-class and middle-class productive citizens are becoming homeless" (National Coalition for the Homeless, 2006).

In December 2006, a report by the United Way of Greater Los Angeles provided insight into the state of women in LA County. The research states that "women face and will continue to face hardship in the decades to come as 40% of families headed by single mothers in LA County are poor. More than a quarter of women 27% in LA County have less than a high school education. 42% of female-headed households pay more than 40% of their income on rent. 22% of women lack any sort of health insurance. Nearly one in five women (18%) lives below the poverty level in LA County" (United Way of Greater Los Angeles, 2006). It is no wonder that there are so many homeless women.

There are countless reasons to study homelessness, but one that stands out in my mind as a parent is the unthinkable number of homeless children in America.

The National Center of Family Homelessness reports that at least "1.35 million U.S. children are homeless and up to 200,000 on any given night during the year." Imagine, "42% of homeless children are under the age of five and requests for emergency shelters by families have increased every year since 1985, with an average increase of 20% in 2002" (National Center of Family Homelessness, 2008). I pray for them.

By now readers understand that some of the causes of homelessness are deep rooted. In fact, The National Coalition for the Homeless reports that nearly "50% of all homeless women and children are fleeing some form of domestic violence. Approximately 25% of the urban homeless are children under 18 and 40% of homeless men have served in the U.S. military and aid to veterans was reduced, so we may in fact see that number grow (Freedom Tracks Music Records, 2008). I have read countless studies and books about homelessness, but what makes this book different is the "raw" time we spent one on one with specific people over an extended period while studying their patterns and behaviors.

As far as social polarity is concerned, I ask my readers, where are all the leaders and role models for our youth? I never thought I would see the day where our youth in disarray, would disrespect authority to the level some do. The past few years has provided Americans with news of one tragedy after the next involving young people shooting their peers and teachers at schools across the country. The Columbine incident is at the top of the list.

All of these social issues contribute to the problem of homelessness and lost unguided people. And, even with proper guidance, our culture allows for these poor choices where in other cultures, homelessness is viewed as "social marginalization" or separate from the homeless problem and seen more of a hardship for people stricken by poverty. In reality, we can't force everyone to take responsibility for his or her life.

Homelessness amongst children is a growing and disturbing trend in the US and throughout the world. I saw one homeless baby with its mother. The mother did not want to be in the book, so I respected her privacy. I met another one, whose parents wanted nothing to do with me.

In 2001, The Urban Institute reported that "3.5 million US residents (about 1% of the population), have been homeless for a significant period of time and in New York alone, there are over 37,000 homeless individuals." In addition, here is the part that really hits me in the gut, enough to get me sick: "16,000 children stay in shelters every night" (Washington Profile, 2004).

On January 2, 2004, New York City's Department of Homeless Services "saw 38,222 homeless people forced to turn to the city's municipal shelter system. Another 1,500 or so beds were filled in churches and other private facilities. Out of this total, at least 16,600 were children, 18 and under" (International Committee of the Fourth International, 2004), showing an increase in childhood homelessness since 2001. Houston, Los Angeles, Louisiana, New York, America, Mission Control…we have a problem. I think you will agree that one homeless child is one too many.

The American family itself has moved away from the stable structure it once proudly displayed. There are also deeper social issues than that of 30 years ago. Drug use is on the rise and our culture is plagued by addictions.

In the drug world, business is booming and there is no recession for Americans. It helps people to hide from their problems rather than face them. There is too much family fighting, AIDS and HIV, the threat of war, and the collapse of business both here and abroad adds to the stressors of the everyday family and their lifestyles. In essence, there are more life events and stressful situations for children, all of which build insecurity in an unstable world. The American family needs to take a second look at the long-term affects of how children suffer when a family falls apart.

Is it just me or can we all agree that childhood should be the happiest time in life, spent having fun playing with other children, going to school, and developing character and skills that prepare our children to hold the great responsibility of building America's future by succeeding in the world?

In the state of Massachusetts, Horizon for Homeless Children reported that in a given year "up to 100,000 children are homeless" (Horizon for Homeless Children, June 2008). When I think of a child being homeless, it breaks my heart. I am sure you know what it feels like to be helpless when you want to help a person, but when the person doesn't want your help, we are forced to look the other way and go about our day. In my mind, it is a good time to change the worldview on these two populations—we are all Americans, including the homeless!

Chapter 25

Dear Diary

Photo: Jane A. Lackner

Best friends Adriana and Brittney as they pose dressed as women.

Of all of the characters in the book, the saddest may very well be one from the Native American culture. The next night after meeting Mark, Kim, Patty, and Eric, as we waited for Mary at our meeting spot on our bench, we were introduced to two of the most interesting and vibrant characters in the book. It was after eight p.m. and Mary was late, but she brought another one of her homeless friends, Adriana, over to meet Jane and me.

Adriana is a thirty-three-year-old Mid-Functioning homeless person originally from Phoenix, Arizona. Adriana is really a man, but we will refer to Adriana as a "she" because that is what he/she prefers to be called.

Adriana has a very outgoing personality and her life is consumed by dramatic interludes, which connect her to a variety of homeless and non-homeless people we meet on the beach. She explains that when she dresses like a woman she is hot. On this night, standing well over six-feet tall, she was wearing a black bandana, jeans, sunglasses, a tank top, and large loop earrings. I also noticed a beautiful necklace Adriana had on that many Native American tribal members wear, made of bone. I asked her if it was tough living out here and how she became homeless and Adriana said, "It's tough with all the drugs around here. I am an alcoholic, but let me tell you something…I was making love to this man on the beach and he had an epileptic seizure so I rolled him over and tried to help him." Then she said that her husband Eric, the man Mary introduced us to the other night, called the lifeguards and they all saved the man. Finally, the paramedics arrived to help the man she was turning a "trick" for in order to buy alcohol. Sure enough, the Los Angeles Fire Department paramedic truck drove past us and Adriana yelled something out to the paramedics inside:

"Bring him back soon!" She said that her lover's medication was stolen and that the hospital will fix him and bring him back to her.

After a few minutes of this crazy story about how Adriana was making love to this man on the beach, her other lover Eric now sat down next to Adriana and was asking for a beer.

Adriana said, "Shut the fuck up," and explained that Eric was no longer her husband, but now was a "has-been."

Mary interrupted because Eric was touching her and trying to kiss her. Mary screamed at Eric, "Get away from me, you're not going to sit there, that is my fucking seat. What are you going to do, hit me?" she asked. Then Mary wanted to move and walked away with Jane.

The drama continued as Adriana went on to tell me that she had to find a means to get what she needed. It is survival. As I asked my next question to Adriana, I was hoping that she could tell me about Coby McBee and the murder, but she did not know him. I had not met a person up to this point who actually was connected to Coby.

Eric then said, "Why was he murdered?" I told them both that Coby was sticking up for some girl and he was stabbed to death. Then Eric said mumbling, but clear enough for me to hear on tape, "Fuck this, you know, one day, I killed the motherfucker before." I said to him, "No, man, you don't know this guy."

I am not sure if Eric could even hurt himself given his drunken state. The twenty times I observed the Mid- to Low-Functioning Eric up and down the beach, he was arguing with himself, talking to the air, and going in and out of personalities.

Then Adriana went into a story about a woman whom she partied with on the beach with four other transsexuals. She said, "My friend heard someone screaming right there [pointing to an area by Marijuana Hill], and lo and behold, what happened…we had our stereo up loud, we heard her screaming, but no one did anything about it until the cops came around."

I asked, "Did she get killed?"

Adriana said, "They killed her because she didn't perform after smoking crack with somebody."

"Did they catch the killer or killers?" I asked.

Adriana looked at me and said, "No, they buried her in the sand, the cops were everywhere. They didn't even bother us." Adriana claims that the woman was a police informant.

I tried to get information on a query, but again, just as when I had questioned the police earlier about why Coby McBee's murder went unpublicized, this murder apparently found the same path.

Eric then chimed in, making no sense, and he said out of nowhere, "You know what the fuck that I was pissed off at him about. You want to hear what the fuck was. It was like, you are going to answer my phone, that's cool, you can, but listen, it is four o'clock in the after-noon." Adriana shut Eric down because he was being dramatic, carrying on a conversation with himself and his invisible friend, and he made absolutely no sense whatsoever.

After Adriana told Eric she was going to bust him over the head with a bottle of beer, she finally silenced him. She revealed much more about her life as drug user and drag queen. Adriana said she was a Crystal-Meth addict who became an alcoholic. Crystal Meth put her on the edge, as it became the downfall in her life. Adriana said she had been clean from the drug for nine months. She also said she used to smoke cocaine. I asked her how a homeless person affords all these drugs. She explained the obvious, that she wasn't always homeless. "I was taking care of my father and I got $20,000 worth of my land money. I spent like $9,000 on Meth, and I was like in and out." The land money Adriana refers to is the money she receives from her Native American tribe that distributes the money evenly to tribe members when they leave the land. The money is accounted for by the council that runs the tribal land.

As Adriana was telling me this story, her husband Eric was trying to hug Mary again. Mary screamed at Adriana to have Eric leave her alone. Mary screamed at Eric, "I don't want to be hugged by you, bitch, you're not my fucking cup of tea." He just kept it up and said to Mary, "Let me have a cigarette." Mary said, "No, bitch, you can't have one, and you don't tell me to get out of the way so that you can be interviewed, I am the star of this book." Mary could not be more correct.

Adriana said she started using Meth in 1998, and to support her habit of drinking and drugging she would go up to men like me, for example, and offer sex for money. She said she made sure the person was not a cop or undercover. She said, "I feel the person out by asking if the person has means to afford to buy drugs, alcohol, or sex." By the end of my tour here, we knew that she was not lying. Some men actually agreed in our presence! She told me she had about seventeen boyfriends on this beach.

As harsh as it sounds, the reality is we watched Adriana live a dangerous game of roulette with the men she entertained. I realize it is not my place to tell people how to live, but Adriana is an intelligent person, and at thirty-two she still could live a productive life if she wanted to. During the time we got to know Adriana, we observed her vomit many times from her alcohol fixation, and knew that only she could change her life. She told us that she had been throwing up in the morning and she had severe alcohol shakes, and a few times, she had even thrown up blood.

While we were sitting on our bench, the now-annoying Eric reappeared, yet again. He mumbled every word that came out of his mouth, but this time I could hear him slur the words "Give me a kiss" to Adriana. At this point, there were too many people whom I did not know who were too close to us, and I really wanted Jane to be safe. We moved into a more open area. One thing about interviewing strangers is that you should always know your surroundings and safety zone.

Then, as I talked to Adriana, another one of Mary's friends came up to say hello because he had not seen her since her release from prison. The man was saying hello to Jane, a petite, beautiful green eyed, long haired brunette. The man was trying to tell her the story about when Mary was on the television show *COPS*. Mary began screaming, "I don't want to hear a story about me, tell her a story about somebody else. I have had a very strenuous day at the welfare office. I have to go to a hotel downtown, so I am not in a good mood. I guess if I give you a blowjob you'll go away." The man then called Mary a "fucking whore" and she said, "Why are you talking to me? Oh, that's right, everybody just disrespects me," and she then punched the man as hard as she could in the shoulder and said, "You fucking-ass bitch. When you start paying my rent and buying my beer, then you can touch my ass." The man remained friendly. Then another man came up at that moment and said, "You got a dime bag?" Mary said, "Bitch, what do I look like, a marijuana dealer? Get the fuck out of my face."

What a night this was turning into!

While all this was going on, Adriana began to tell Jane about the "mis-decongestion of alcoholism and best friends. It's the contradiction, it's the best friend you can have, but as long as you laugh through it you can probably get through it."

The most important aspect of Adriana's life is her Native American heritage. Her family and culture mean so much to her. They define who she is. There is a much deeper, interesting side to her. Adriana told us that her mother had been an alcoholic prior to Adriana's birth and then stopped when she was born. After her children grew old enough to leave the home, her mother went back to drinking profusely and eventually became addicted to alcohol again.

It was well past midnight now, but Adriana went on about her childhood.

Adriana has some sad memories growing up. She was in a situation where a group of men beat her and her lover pretty badly. They busted a television over her head and punched her face in so badly that it left many visible scars on her face. Then they robbed her and the lover and left her for dead. Because of her sexual preference, she has been ridiculed throughout her life, but in the Native American tribe of the Sioux, Adriana keeps a very low profile as to her sexual preference so that her family is not embarrassed, she said. Face work or public image is very important in Native America culture. A family's reputation is developed through the reputation of the parents. So being gay is not something easily revealed by Adriana.

A much greater problem Adriana admits is alcoholism. Adriana's biggest challenge is overcoming her own alcoholism. Living the tribal life requires discipline and respect. Adriana, while not a disrespectful person, needed an escape from the pressure of trying to live up to the expectations of others' demands in the tribe.

There was a time in Adriana's life when she went into Job Corp, which is a government outreach program offered by the U.S. Department of Labor, where she had the opportunity to complete an education, learn a marketable trade, make lifetime friends, and graduate with a good job. Things didn't work out because at the time Adriana was going through a lot at home with her family. Prior to that, she became sexually involved with a relative, which brought about tribal conflict. The traditional Native American rules prohibit homosexuality in tribal culture, leaving Adriana exposed. The relative was very abusive toward her and a number of other women, and he was addicted to Crystal as well.

As Adriana opened up to Jane, I listened to how her life changed drastically. The only figure Adriana truly respected was her mother. Adriana told Jane that when her mother died, it was a blow that devastated her. She still had not recovered from the loss of her mother and cried as she spoke of the day of her mother's funeral. One of the patterns I noticed developing was that the homeless who have had hardships have had difficulties managing their lives and overcoming the loss of loved ones, unable to find the inner strength to carry on a productive lifestyle. Adriana said, "I never knew my mother was so respected on that level. My mother had so many star quilts, and traditional beautiful quilts. Oh my god! The flowers lined up this way and that way." She said that in her tribe "people who had nothing made something for her funeral" because they respected her mother so much. They went into the forest and got wild berries and anything that represented nature and the spirit in which her mother lived her life. She said, "When I got close to her casket, I lifted her veil up, she had gold on her glasses, with all her wings on, all her jewelry on, and all black gold. I had nothing to give her and I knew that it would be disrespectful if I left nothing, so I took my gold bracelet off and they [tribe members] told me not to touch her. I just leaned over and put the bracelet on her, lifted her head up, and I kissed her on the forehead."

In true fashion, Adriana rebelled, but we have to understand that different cultures handle death in other ways. Adriana tried to hold onto the one person who believed in her. She said she loved her mother and her mother loved her unconditionally.

Adriana's uncles, cousins, and tribal members all attended a beautiful funeral. She said, "They were cooking two cows outside, the men were there, but the cows were so beautiful. I actually saw them carve the cows and it was just so dramatic." Years ago, Adriana said, "I saw my mom carve her own cow and I helped her carve it when she was healthy and she did her ceremony for the sun dance. I watched them blow the cow's head off and kill the cow. I saw all the beautiful old ladies with their knives down by the river to help carve the cow."

Jane asked Adriana what her mother's last words were to her. She said, "I called her and my mother said, 'Why are you drinking?' I didn't respond." Instead, Adriana just listened. Then Adriana said that at the funeral, "When I am in that van alone and everybody's gone and

I am sitting there waiting for Francis, which is Francis One Feather, there is a lady who appears from nowhere and she is talking to me. She continued, 'Mom, that is a fucking double and she is such an evil person.'" Jane then asked her what happened next. She replied, "I said to my mother, 'Stop,' and my mother said, 'My baby is going to be okay.'" The way that Adriana explains it, this double that she saw is apparently a two-sided spirit that was talking to her. The spirit represents good versus evil. That presence appeared again to Adriana after the death of her mother.

Adriana took us into the vortex of what tore her life apart as she continued to find hope and a reason to live. Her mother played such an important role in her life. Oftentimes we find ourselves asking questions that we do not know the answers to. Life is not beautiful for all of us. Sometimes, though, I thought to myself, we have to channel as much positive energy as we can in light of the challenges we face.

Nurturing ourselves by surrounding ourselves with positive and uplifting people who care about us helps us to look past our problems and focus on any promise for the future. We can only hope that for the time we touched Adriana's life, she will remember the positive guidance we provided by listening to something she felt the urge to share.

Most of us grow when we lose people. It helps us to put life's problems into perspective. Self-discovery is an important part of life because it helps us to relate to other people. While I have a positive attitude in life, I understand and realize that not everyone can be like me. I remember days when doctors told us that it could go either way with my own son's battle with leukemia, but I never shared this at the time with Adriana because it was her moment, her time to pour her heart out to us. Instead, Jane and I just hugged her.

As I examined the success I was having getting people to open up to me through other people, I continued to hone my communication skills in becoming an expert talking to various homeless people who possess different communication styles and come from all walks of life.

I must say that our hearts were broken listening to Adriana. The more homeless people I communicated with, the more my confidence in building relationships with them grew, but it also meant that I would be hearing stories that were hard to listen to.

This much I know: in order to work on being open-minded, communicating with the homeless is very different from conducting a business meeting or lecturing in the classroom. It takes patience and critical listening skills. As for evaluating a conversation, that depends on whom you may be talking to, such as a High-, Mid-, or Low-Functioning homeless person. Obviously, each person is different. Like a Vegas show, next up this evening Eric, Adriana's former husband or boyfriend, comes back to the bench with his sleeping bag wrapped around his naked body as he exposes his genitals from the draping bag, searching for his lover and so-called wife, Adriana.

 Chapter 26

Brittany: A Walk on the Wild Side

Photo: Jane A. Lackner
Brittany takes the mask of fun and games off and gets serious.

Days later, Adriana showed up with her other friend, Brittany. At second look, we realized that Brittany was actually a man. She was close to six feet tall, had very long blonde hair and blue eyes, was muscularly thin, but had a deceiving appearance when she dressed like a woman. Like Adriana, Brittany is a man who says he wants to be known as a woman. She is a thirty-two-year-old Mid-Functioning transsexual, originally from Arkansas. Before arriving to Venice Beach by bus, Brittany lived in Florida and Louisiana.

The first time we met Brittany, she was very friendly, had no shirt on, and was tan, and she was showing us a sexual gesture with her mouth using a banana.

Brittany was quite funny when the mask was on, but that was only because she did not know us, nor did she trust us at first. When the mask came off, however, we became acquainted with one of the most sensitive, caring people you could ever meet. She showed us a different side of life that, again, is unpopular in American culture: homosexuality.

Brittany has had a life filled with drama. Being one of eight children is never easy, but her parents were successful. Her mother owns a business and her father was a military man, who after his service in the military also became successful in business.

When Brittany dresses up in drag and puts her lipstick and makeup on, she can pass for a female. Brittany and Adriana allowed us inside their world and lifestyle. Jane and I have never been judgmental of this lifestyle because we both have many friends who are gay, who are productive, positive people just like us. We look at both Adriana and Brittany openly, with an objective mind, and as people with feelings first.

Spending more than a month of every day talking to Brittany led to her opening up to us. I could feel deep down that Brittany wanted to talk, but she wasn't sure she could trust. I find that people by nature like to talk about their lives especially if the situation and company are right. My goal was to make it feel right for Brittany so that eventually she would open a side of her life up to us that she might not have ordinarily. I wanted her story to be told or as much of it as I could gather.

Actually, it was Jane who paved the way. The night Jane asked the girls jokingly if she could do a photo shoot of them dressed up as women, they began opening up. Adriana and Brittany loved the idea. This was the first time they felt accepted by Jane. It showed we accepted them for who they were and they realized this.

It took weeks before Brittany decided to share her story. When I asked questions, early on she would reply, "You're digging." She now told us that she was a person trapped in a life filled with alcohol and drug addiction. We learned to care about her as she cried through her despair in telling us the painful true stories of her life as a teenager and homeless person. In fact, Adriana and Brittany parked their outdoor hotel right next to the lifeguard stand on the beach. Their bags, which they left on the beach overnight, were thrown out by the beach sanitation patrol and they lost most of their belongings that day.

Brittany has been homeless for seven years. She is a person who has suffered in life because of the feelings that many gay people feel having been teased he entire childhood for having feminine characteristics. In our society, she said she just wants to be loved and not judged. Even as a youngster, she had to hide her true self in order to be accepted in both her family and society. She has not talked to her mother in a long time, leaving her mother with the question, is she dead or alive?

She said that her mother is most likely brokenhearted not knowing where Brittany is. Brittany does not call her mother because she does not want to upset her with the knowledge that she is living on the beach as a homeless person. As a result, Brittany drinks to take away life's pain.

While it is hard to understand why someone like Brittany lives this homeless lifestyle, she sounds like she is giving up and feels hopeless, helpless, and disrespected by people. This emotion can twist a person's self-concept, particularly a person living the life she lives where there is so much hate and bias toward gay people. I could never understand this society and how people just love to live their own life through the lives of others. Let people be themselves and let it go already. If it were a perfect world, we would have no homeless and this book would reveal nothing.

From a parent's perspective, Brittany's broken life was devastating as she took us through the details about the poor choices she admitted she had made in her life. She said that her main concern was to eat and survive, and run away from her own inner conflict in order to find peace.

Brittany and Adriana are both very nice people. They have every right to be whom they choose to be. They are no different from you or me when it comes to finding happiness. After all, who among us is perfect?

Switching gears here for a second, the only thing that concerned me as a friend of Adriana and Brittany was that they could be potential victims of a hate crime, and I worried about their health. Brittany had mentioned that six "skin-heads" who allegedly were "haters" of gay people wanted to beat her up and that she would stand and fight. It was not my business, but I advised her to run to the police up the walk if that happened.

Since Jane and I were outsiders in their world, I did realize that the dangers in mixing with people we really did not know continued to grow. My gut instincts told me that the couple would be interesting to talk to because they are open-minded, thought-provoking, and proud of who they are. We respect that. As for the dangers in being around strangers, it becomes more dangerous when you pry into their lives because people get this way through things that may be very painful to talk about and it can ignite feelings that fill them with anger and rage. Regardless, in the back of my mind, I see the bigger picture and use the opportunity as a chance to help people see themselves better so that there is the small chance they redefine their life's purpose. Failure and quitting is not something I take lightly in my own life.

As for the health safety issue, Adriana and Brittany told us they recently had been tested for HIV, and are not HIV-positive. HIV and AIDS are scary things.

I remember being an intern with Earl Ubell, former health and science reporter for WCBS-TV Channel 2 News, in New York City in the summer of 1989, when I was exposed to the word "AIDS." I was petrified with what I saw, and since that hot summer day when we interviewed intravenous drug users who knew nothing about HIV and AIDS, I concluded that all the people that Ubell had interviewed that day, in all probability, were no longer here. They shared needles at the peak of the AIDS crisis in this country.

Just last week August 24, 2008, New York legislators and the governor cut $427 million from the budget that will affect many needy New Yorkers. For the truly needy this is wrong. The reductions will impact HIV/AIDS treatment, Medicaid funding, community health centers, social services and other programs that serve the poor.

In Los Angeles County "11,323 have AIDS, 10,954 are living, and 369 have died as a result of the disease as of September 30, 2008" (California Department of Public Health, 2008). While Adriana and Brittany maintain that they have tested negative for the HIV virus, their probability of acquiring HIV and AIDS increases, especially given their promiscuous lifestyle.

From an academic perspective, any students who want to study psychology, or observe people with behaviors different from themselves, should visit Venice Beach to do their observations—they would meet every type of person imaginable. I am sure that all the knowledge the psychology students learn in the classroom can be applied to what is observed firsthand here on Venice Beach. For graduate students, go homeless for a few weeks with the homeless and your lesson will turn into a thesis paper for graduate school. Just know when to stay out of harm's way and inform the police as to what you are doing so that they are aware that if you need a security anchor, the beach police are only a phone call away.

Brittany told me that she had been in and out of prison for prostitution and at one point spent nearly two years in jail. One of the stories that Brittany allowed us to share was the story about how while in jail she met a man she fell in love with. Upon their release, she would stay at his house on and off and tell her new boyfriend's girlfriend that the boyfriend could not see her on certain days so that Brittany could spend time with him. Then she worked for a gay professor who wrote math and science texts. She said she was his gopher working stressful hours until finally she decided the gig was up serving the professor. I actually had an inspiring conversation with Brittany. She respected me by the time we left, as she told me with tears running down her face, "I just want to say that at first I didn't trust you, but now I realize that your intentions are good and that you are a really good person, I was wrong about you." This is just another lesson in perception.

As I sit here and write this, I realize that my life goes back to structure in New York, and sadly, Brittany's life remains in the dark depths of chaos on Venice Beach. My promise to Brittany is that there are certain things that I will not write about that she told me because they are just too painful and private. Protecting her dignity is more important than getting the dramatic story.

Saying goodbye to Brittany left me thinking that I could help her to get her life back on track, but then I realized that it is not my place to lecture someone like her about making life changes; she knows that already.

 **Chapter 27**

The Masks of Homeless

Most people present themselves differently in each communication episode, wearing a variety of masks to match the mood, situation, and event of the interpersonal encounter. For the homeless the mask is usually off because you see them in one of the most difficult of circumstances, revealing their self-concept openly. There is no hidden behavior; it's out in the open.

When we have our mask on, we use that opportunity to make a public impression of how we want people to see us, and we are generally guarded. Most of the time, we want to leave people with a positive impression of who we are. For example, our behaviors at work may not be the same behaviors we display in the presence of friends or family. Even animals wear masks. We have a male cat that was very submissive around the other male cat who was the boss in the house. As soon as the dominant male cat died, within a week the animal's instincts kicked in and he changed from being submissive to become a dominant and aggressive animal that terrorized the female cat in the house. We never saw this cat taking the dominant role before and he even stayed on the second floor of the house for a year until that other male died.

When we get to know a person, the mask comes off and a person's true personality comes out, and we sometimes get to know the person at the deepest levels of his or her personality. We learn this as we begin to trust, feel more comfortable with, and build relationships with people to the point that we can take the mask off and be our true selves.

Sometimes we let our guard down, allowing those we trust, such as friends, family, lovers, and others, inside our comfort zone, and we get hurt or even hurt others. Usually, when our mask is off, the people who know us best know our most revealing behaviors. The interesting component to this mask on- and offstage is that on the outside we only know what we see and hear, so we may make judgments about other people's honesty. From Adriana and Brittany, we learned over time that they are two very honest people who are struggling with their addictions and society's objection to their lifestyle.

A few nights after meeting Adriana and Brittany, as we sat on our bench after nine p.m., I explained to Mary, Adriana, and Brittany that we all wear masks. Under the mask are behaviors either consistent or inconsistent with whom we present ourselves as in public. Mary says, "Fuck the mask theory, I DON'T WEAR NO FUCKING MASK, BITCH, and FUCK YOU PROFESSOR." I replied, "Mary, you make me feel disrespected as a professor, so lose the label. I prefer Bo."

In reality, this mask theory is true in nearly everyone's life. My point is that in public, Adriana presents herself as a flighty, free-spirited, transvestite gay male, but when Adriana takes the mask off, there is a compassionate person stuck in deep emotional thought and conflict. Adriana asked me why she was so bitter and I told her that we all have a cross to bear, but bitterness only harms the heart. Heal your heart I told her. "Love yourself, let go of the hate, and find a way to use the peace within your soul to rest the heartaches you have had."

Adriana just smiled and said, "Dear Diary."

Chapter 28

The Self-Proclaimed Vampire of Venice

Tommy C. Manson Talks!

Photo: Jane A. Lackner

Self-proclaimed Vampire Tommy Manson or Va, as he lurks around at the same pail at the same time each night.

Tommy is back! Some things will never change. Tommy was wearing the exact clothing we saw him in a year ago and he is still a creature of habit that showed up at the same time doing the same things every day and night. He sat in the same spot on a hill I call the "grassy knoll," near Muscle Beach all day until it was time for him to make his garbage-pail stops every night by our homeless bench at the same time, between eight thirty p.m. and nine p.m.

One evening as we sat on our bench with Mary, who now meets us every night religiously at seven p.m. to converse with us, Tommy walked by. He was holding the usual coffee cup in his hand as he picked through the garbage pail. Tonight he found a spoon in the garbage, looked at it, and put it back in the garbage pail.

As we watched him, Mary started in about Tommy being a Charlie Manson disciple and anarchist, so she decided to yell at him from a few feet away, "Hey, Tommy, you Charlie Manson's fucking disciple, you're not going to kill us, are you bitch, you fucking anarchist? And did you cut that baby out of Sharon Tate too, bitch?" Mary continued to ramble on, screaming, "You are the devil, bitch, why is it that you have to come down here in my territory and try to fuck with people, you fucking anarchist." I just looked at this scene in shock, and said to myself, "It's a madhouse." Jane was speechless. Just as he had in the past, Tommy C. Manson said nothing as he walked away.

Actually, I was praying that Tommy did not answer. This behavior eventually would warrant a response. Jane said to me, "I hope he doesn't have a good memory and remember who we are because of what Mary thinks about him." A second later, another man who was a vendor who stayed further down the beach playing heavy metal guitar and singing, rode by on his bike, which had an attachment carrying all of his belongings. The man has long dark hair past his shoulders, wears a bandana to hold his hair in place and has on dirty blue jeans, a dirty t-shirt, and sneakers. Mary began to yell at him as well. She said, "Well, look who it is, bitch, another Manson disciple." The man said nothing and just looked at Mary. She then yelled, "Listen, bitch, don't you know it is a fine if you ride your fucking bike on the walk here, asshole?" The man rode off. I could not stop laughing because television entertainment cannot compare to this stuff.

Weeks later, Jane and I were walking to where Tommy sits on the grassy knoll across from the tattoo parlor off of Brook Street when we saw him sitting writing in a notebook. There were thousands of people walking on the gorgeous sunny day and it was about seventy-five degrees. We were walking back from a free concert on the beach performed by R&B recording artist NE-YO. I was carrying my camera and tape recorder to take photos and interview people for the book when I came up with this brilliant idea. I said to Jane, "I would love to take a photo of Tommy C. Manson for the front cover of my book in order to present a 'faithful comprehensive depiction' of the homeless for my nonverbal studies," but I knew I wouldn't be able to use a photo of his face in the book without his signing a release.

At least I could show my students a slide show in the fall on homelessness and they could see the Low-Functioning Tommy's picture. Jane decided that she wanted to volunteer to go take a close-up of

Tommy. That was a terrible mistake. Tommy went ballistic. As Jane was shooting photos, I was a nervous onlooker. Tommy was looking all over the place and his eyes slowly followed Jane, who had the camera in her hand, trying to act inconspicuous, when suddenly Tommy began a tirade and screamed at the top of his lungs to Jane, "Fucking bitch, get away from me, bitch. I am gonna cut you into tomorrow land, you fucking bitch. Motherfucker, I am gonna cut you up." This was the first time Tommy spoke and he just kept screaming. Then a man walked past him and Tommy yelled at the top of his lungs to him, "Get the fuck away from me. I'll kill you all." As Jane left quickly, we listened to Tommy continue to yell at the world and at anyone and everyone. I am honestly not sure if Tommy was reacting to Jane's taking his photo, or because he wanted no one near him in his stage of paranoia. For a few minutes, it was a scary and a tense scene to see someone react so violently to something so insignificant. Suffice to say, Jane left the scene beyond scared.

Call me crazy, but I am fascinated by what makes the mind tick and why people act the way they do. Imagine, a man in his fifties can spend his entire life living in another dimension like this. He is free to roam about the universe and fend for himself without any help if he chooses to. I wish I could help Tommy, but I think, sadly, that he is beyond reach.

A week later, while Jane and I took a walk, we saw Tommy on the grassy knoll again in the same exact spot, writing in his notebook, when on a dare Jane asked me to go sit with Tommy. I love a challenge, and I was sincerely determined and curious to get to know Tommy from a psychological perspective as a study for this book, in order to remove Mary's stereotype of who she believed Tommy was. She almost had us believing that Tommy was an anarchist, but I knew better. I decided that I would in fact walk right up to Tommy and sit next to him man to man on his turf to learn anything I could about him.

As I walked up to Tommy I was a little nervous, but I felt that this could be the last chance I had to talk to Tommy before leaving Venice Beach. Besides, I knew I could outrun him if I had to. So I sat down right next Tommy and said to him, "Hey, how are you today? It is a hot day, isn't it?" He said, in a very soft-spoken and articulate manner, "Why, yes, it is." I was shocked! "Mind if I sit down?" I asked. He replied, "Not at all, it is free space." I was beyond surprised that Tommy actually was friendly and out of character from the week before.

In conducting an interview, I try to be as unobtrusive as possible, and interview as though I am a psychology student so that I can learn as much as I can in a short period of time from a subject. Since I worked as a reporter for fourteen years, I thought that I had a knack for being persistent and stubborn, and I developed a reputation for getting the news from tough sources working for one of the largest publishing companies in the world. I wasn't going to quit talking to Tommy, but for once, I was at a loss for words.

Jane was sitting directly across from the grassy knoll overlooking the beach. It was my turn in the spotlight. I was wearing my sunglasses and I could see Jane in my peripheral vision motioning for me to remove my glasses. I had the biggest smile on my face as I looked at her because I knew that I had won an unauthorized interview with Tommy C. Manson.

When I am talking to someone, I also have this bad habit of keeping my sunglasses on. It is rude. Therefore, I removed the glasses and made direct eye contact with Tommy. As I looked into Tommy's bright blue eyes I forgot to ask one of the most important questions of Tommy: "What is your name?" It was obvious that Tommy had no recollection of who Jane and I were in light of the fact that he wanted to kill her days earlier for taking his photo.

Instead of asking Tommy his name, I asked him a different question. I asked him if he knew crazy Mary. He said yes and that Mary Philbin is a writer and actress and she was a star in the movie *Dracula* in the 1920s. I checked, and actually Philbin was a star in *The Phantom of the Opera* in the 1920s. Tommy said, "She now sews and weaves all the hats here on the beach, and she was in the moon and stars at night in case you don't know that. But, more important are the night creatures on this beach you know...we are surrounded by Vampires. And, by the way take note of all of the living Vampires that live among us. Praise them, rejoice them, embrace them, they won't bite you." Okay, this was getting scary. Was this guy going to turn on me?

213

His eyes had a crazed look in them as they looked like they shook in the orbit of the eye.

I thought, I am now lost again, but at this minute I was so happy to talk to Tommy and even happier that he didn't mind my sitting to talk with him that I looked at Jane and nodded for her to come over and sit with us, but first I asked Tommy for his permission and he approved.

When Jane came over, she immediately introduced herself and then asked Tommy for his name. He paused and said, "Ah, yes, my name is…Va, yes." Looking closer at Va, I noticed his front two teeth were rotten and he had two cigarettes in his hand, which he had picked up from the ground. I then asked Va how long he had lived on Venice and he told me two years. It was exhausting trying to keep up with Va because he rambled in and out of different characters and subjects as many times as we blink our eyes.

In a state of anxiety, Va went right back on the topic of Mary and began telling us that she lived on the beach. He also told us that he was trying to escape the voices that were talking to him. I looked up the symptoms of schizophrenia and within the definition, it said that people with the illness may hear voices, have paranoid thoughts, and talk to themselves using various voices. The next day I walked up to Va the Venice Vampire to say hello. He replied, "Fuck you, get away from me."

In the United States, "more than 2 million Americans suffer from schizophrenia compared to the United Kingdom where "roughly

487,483 of the 60 million people in the UK suffer from the disease" (Wrong Diagnosis.com, 2008).

Mental Health America, or MHA, states that "only one-third of individuals seek treatment" for the disease. The toll of mental illness is enormous. MHA reports that "one in five Americans suffers from a diagnosable mental illness in a given year. Four of the ten leading causes of disability worldwide are mental disorders. Among developed nations, including the United States, major depression is the leading cause of disability. Also near the top of these rankings are manic-depressive illness, schizophrenia, and obsessive-compulsive disorder. The direct cost of mental health services, which includes spending for treatment and rehabilitation, is approximately $69 billion in the United States. Indirect costs, which refer to lost productivity at the workplace, school, and home, are estimated at $78.6 billion" (Mental Health America of Eastern Missouri, 2008).

We don't know if Va has used any drugs in his life, but Reuters recently reported a study that "using marijuana increases the risk of one day developing a psychotic illness such as schizophrenia." The study "provides some of the strongest evidence yet linking the drug to a mental disorder. But this study marks one of the most comprehensive, thorough and reliable reviews of its kind and should serve as a warning, two Danish researchers wrote in an accompanying comment in the Lancet medical journal" (Reuters, 2007). Non-medicinal marijuana is one of the most commonly used illegal substances here on Venice Beach and in the United States.

After Va told me that actress Mary Philbin, who died in 1993, and Stevie Nicks, rock singer from the band Fleetwood Mac, were the same person, he went on to tell me that he studied Voodoo and loved the horror genre. He also said that he was a vampire. He was dead serious. I asked him if there were a lot of drugs on the beach and he said that Mary Philbin did many mushrooms or LSD, which was why she was such a good actress. He seemed obsessed with Mary Philbin, who perhaps was terrorizing him, I thought, but because of his mental state, maybe someone else would be terrorizing Va in his mind tomorrow. We'll never know.

Va then noticed the rings I was wearing. One was my college ring, which is a nice gold ring with green emerald stone, and the other was a ring that I had bought here in Venice that had little Hawaiian flowers on it. Va said that my flower ring could get me into the Catholic Church while my college ring would get me into England to meet the Queen. Talking very fast, Va said the ring represented royalty, unlike his skull ring, which he said represented the devil, but it would get him to meet other vampires. Obviously, I could not laugh at what Va said because then he would think I was making fun of him, and since he was unpredictable, I thought it best to stay neutral.

Va again went back to the Mary Philbin story and complimented Jane on her lavender bracelet and me on my sandals and my tan. We then began talking about something pertaining to the country and the military and Jane asked him if he had served. Va said that he served in the Navy Air Force in Vietnam, but he didn't seem sure. I thought to myself, *Okay, which one?* Va had no concept of reality. I asked Va if I could buy him some food, but he told me that the food was poisoned here, so no, I could not buy him food. This again showed the paranoia part of his schizophrenia. "Do you know today's date," I asked? Va replied, "Sure, it's January 1997." Actually, the correct date was July 4, 2008.

After nearly twenty minutes of talking to Va, I told him it was great to meet him and I asked him if he wanted some clothes before we headed back to New York. Va said, "Thanks, but no thanks, you probably have fleas." *I have fleas?* I thought.

While Va obviously wanted nothing to do with society, I could not help but think about what he feels and goes through each day wandering about, but I was pleased to learn more about what makes people in his condition tick. The scary thing is they are just out here existing with no way back into a stable and productive lifestyle. We finally met the Venice Beach Vampire!

Chapter 29

Mary: Life in the Fast Lane

Living life to the fullest, the next morning I took my usual jog from our place on the beachfront to the Santa Monica Pier and back. It is a peaceful, invigorating way to begin my day. Many people get to know me and I love the fact that my home away from home brings new people into my life.

Mary caught me after my run at our bench and normal meeting spot and told me she was "5150ed." which is the LAPD's code for taking a subject into custody for being a danger either to herself or to others. By this time, Mary felt so comfortable with us and I could tell she really looked up to me. She said she looked at me like a son and that I was everything she wished she could be.

I asked how this all came about. Mary's 5150 landed her in the hospital overnight, and when I saw her, she looked very drug-induced from the medication the psych ward at the hospital gave her. Mary, said, "I was sitting in the middle of the road on the yellow line on Main Street, and there were 'clowns on the left, and jokers on the right, and I was stuck in the middle' because I didn't know what to do. Suddenly, two jeeps pulled up. A man got out of one and a woman got out of another, and God told me that these two people were pedophiles so I called the police and I was taken away as a 5150 by the police."

There is a crazy logic to some of Mary's actions. In Mary's mind, she uses a lot of music to connect and make sense of her life. To us, it may seem illogical, but to Mary, sitting in the middle of the road to draw attention to herself so that she can receive treatment and have a safe place to sleep makes total sense.

Later that night at our usual meeting spot, Mary showed us the discharge sheet, which explained to us the purpose of Mary's psychiatric evaluation for being a danger to herself and others. The report also showed that she had been given numerous medications, as evidenced by her squinting eyes. She seemed sedated and very calm.

One thing is certain: Mary has survived all the fights in the dark and is still going strong, but several times, she said that she was going to kill herself because she said she was growing tired of the world. A few hours later, Mary began drinking and I was a little disappointed in her because her father living in Kentucky had just sent her a money order for $68. She had picked it up from her friend whom she has mail sent to, who gave her the letter and the money order. Within five minutes of opening the letter from her father, Mary spent $27 on a sweatshirt that was too small and the rest on cigarettes and beer. I told Mary, "Why don't you save your money, Mary, so that you can buy food and other things?"

Jane reminded me that it is important not to tell Mary what to do. I guess I realized how I must have sounded to Mary giving her orders. It is, after all, her life, and after a while, a person can become attached to a homeless person, and what may be rational to me may be irrational to her. That does not mean that Mary is not intelligent, because she is. It just comes down to the difference between the choices I would make and the choices Mary makes by continuing to drink alcohol and losing her self-control as she gets intoxicated. When Mary loses self-control that is when she gets in the most trouble. We didn't want to see her back in jail, but going back to jail seems inevitable for Mary.

On a lighter note, Mary is a natural-born comedian. It was ten p.m. and a group of roughly fifteen businesslike people, all men with attaché cases, were in a circle literally ten feet from our bench as they were scouting the vicinity for what we overhear them saying was "a romantic spot for a night shoot" on the beach. These people really were Hollywood people and I thought they knew natural talent, but apparently, they didn't find much humor in Mary. Mary walked right in between them, looking them up and down, and said to the group, "Who the fuck is in charge here bitch? I need a good attorney. Are any of you assholes an attorney?" A group of confused and shocked faces looked at Mary and they explained what they were doing in her spot. "Why the fuck are you all dressed up here on Venice Beach…[she looks up and down at a very tall man in the group]…I think you should get the fuck off the beach and go back to Hollywood pecker head," she said. The group quickly moved away from Mary's spot as she continued to shout obscenities at them. "Let me shout what everyone else wants to tell you Hollywood assholes, but they are afraid. You all care about your own selfish asses, bitch. Get lost. Don't come back, this is Venice Beach not Hollywood."

Mary is territorial and she does not want other people to talk to us on "her" time. Jane and I become the hand that provides the proper emotional support Mary requires, but Mary wants Jane and me to herself, and she gets very upset when we talk to others. I told Mary she would never make it in New York because I talk to hundreds of people each day and my office hours are booked every semester. She would be cursing at my students. The territorial thing that Mary has also applies to her piece of the real estate on Venice Beach, which is our meeting spot. If someone approaches, she says, "Fuck off, bitch."

Mary then walks back to the group again and starts in. She said to the group as she looked up at them, "I need a good fucking attorney to get me out of all the trouble I am in. Now, get the fuck out of here if you can't help me." The pain of getting the story sometimes, I thought. I walked over to Mary, making eye contact with the group, and because this was her second time walking in the circle between the group it was time to move her along so I said, "Mary, come with me it is time to eat dinner." Then we walked back to our bench, but as soon as we did a few of the people in the group said, "Okay, we are leaving, don't worry about it." Mary replied, "Good, go the fuck back to Hollywood, you assholes." I thought, *there goes my chance to be a movie star.*

In a way, I thought Mary spoke for the public and the way I personally feel about the phony Hollywood scene, but these were nice people. Mary has the nerve to tell people the things you or I may be afraid to say. As one passerby dressed in Lederhosen looked at her a few minutes after the Hollywood people left, Mary yelled at the man, "Go back to Hollywood, you fairy."

This never-ending cycle of instability continues to put Mary on the brink of trouble.

Part 6

Chapter 30

Joel: In Search Of His Destiny

Weeks pass by and Mary is back out on the street after clearing up her parole violation. We were talking to Adriana when she introduced me to a former homeless man, Joel. The night is young and the company remains interesting with the best to come.

Joel is a thirty-two-year-old man from Mexico City, Mexico, who pulled up on his BMX bicycle, smiling at Jane and me, and then politely introduced himself. Joel has been all over America. He has been to Seattle, North Carolina, Georgia, Tennessee, Kentucky, New York, and a host of other states before landing on Venice Beach.

Joel is a very talkative man. He is a great role model for the struggling homeless young men in this country. He learned through hardships, wanted better for himself, and has turned himself into a self-made man by working hard to get results. He said when he came from Mexico City to New York seven years ago, he was eating out of the garbage pails for five months during the winter on 42nd Street and Lexington Avenue, freezing his ass off, and then he lowered himself to beg in the subways in order to survive.

Joel was very informative, telling me that after midnight, Dudley turns into a drug area. He said, "They smoke crack, but if you no do drug, es no problemo." However, I already knew that and I had no reason not to believe him. He seemed honorable and showed me his Mexican military identification, which he still carries with pride. What I loved most about Joel was his survival skills, drive, positive attitude, and endurance. Like many people from other third-world cultures, he is such a proud person. He served two years in the military and bragged about the six identifications he carried from grammar school on up to the military where he perfected the skill of being a soldier.

Like many of my students in New York, here we have a man who has turned his life completely around and said he looks back at life from another level now. While he is not making big money, he lives within his comfort level and affords things here that he could never afford in Mexico City. The point is that Joel is working hard to achieve his vision of the American Dream, as he puts life into perspective. He said he has been able to make more of himself now than if he were in Mexico or living homeless on the mean streets of New York because he is a survivor. I asked him what gave him the inspiration to change. In broken English, with a Spanish accent, Joel said that suddenly something clicked in his head and God told him not to break his spirit and pride. Joel took the risk and never allowed the curse from birth of being poor and struggling to get the best of his principles. He said he knew that he would be dead if he stayed in the gutters of New York. If it were not for a cousin who gave him an "honor loan," which was enough to get him out of the cold harsh environment of New York and out west to Los Angeles by bus, Joel said again, he would be dead. This attitude is one that many of the other homeless people we met are missing.

Mary arrives and then interrupted and began talking to Joel. She said, "Why are you here bitch? I have never seen you before." I interjected and said, "Mary, maybe he is just strolling the beach like the thousands of other people here." She said, "Would you be quiet without interjection while I conduct this interview, Bo."

Joel said, "It is my off day today, so I am relaxing." Mary said, "I have been off all day too, motherfucker. We could have been together all day." Joel then began talking about how he liked to watch television. He said it gave him relief with his tight schedule. Mary said, "Do you like watching pornographic movies?" Joel said, "I never see because I stay inside of my apartment and I am usually tired." I interrupted and said, "Okay, Mary, you are fired." Mary then asked Joel, "Do you believe in sex before marriage?" Joel said in his broken accented English, "I don't marry, I am not married." I told Mary to stop and she said, "As you can see, my mind is in the sexual mode. I would not corrupt him." She then asked Joel if he would marry her. Joel said, "I hope so, maybe." I said to Joel, "You don't understand." Mary continued, "I need a man with a home and a job and a television, and washing machine." I said, "Yeah, Joel, you don't need a person who has been in jail almost two hundred times."

When he came to Venice, Joel secured a job at Gold's Gym working endless hours to honor the agreement to pay back his cousin. He has been working there for six years. After his debt was paid, he began working a second job at a Beverly Hills supermarket, which caters to the rich and famous. It takes him more than an hour each day by bus to get to that job.

Mary said to Joel, "You are too good to be true." Joel said, "I am not allowed to use drugs because I get drug-tested for my job working in Beverly Hills." Joel continued, "Do you know, I see Jennifer Lopez. She buys $1,500 in food at the market." I answered, "Wow! That food will last her forever." Joel had a way of knowing what was best for him and strove to make better choices with his life.

Joel now works twelve to fourteen hours a day, every day of the week, and he has secured an apartment that he shares, and now has greater hope for his future. Joel is one of the few great success stories of going from the homeless lifestyle to being a productive citizen. He attributes his success to the military discipline and his own personal pride, something no one can ever take away from him. He never allowed being homeless to break him. Joel said that Mexico is a different culture and although it is very poor, people respect the law and others. In the United States, he said that he feels people look down on him. Joel said, "Americans should only know how tough life is in other parts of the world."

In California, Joel talked about the gang violence and people he avoids, calling them "the pitfalls of American society." He loves America, he said, but he feels that people are lazy sometimes. For example, his roommate had friends over to their apartment last month and $800 was missing from Joel's pants pocket. He said he thinks that the roommate and the roommate's friend stole the money while he slept, but that he could not prove this. Instead of becoming violent, Joel said that money is something he can make back as he has learned by fighting his way back in life and into the light. Again, Joel's outlook on life after what he has already lived through is an admirable lesson we can all learn from. He said he kept his head up by working extra hours to make up for the lost money. I was inspired by Joel and thought, *Why can't everyone who is homeless be like hardworking Joel?*

Chapter 31

Kazou

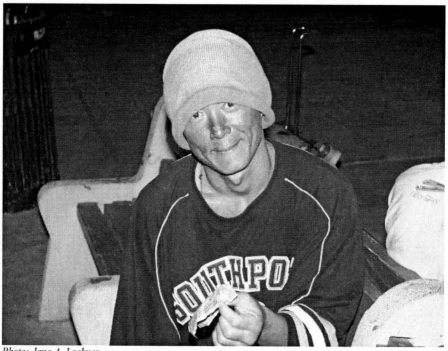

Photo: Jane A. Lackner
Japanese Native, Kazou pays back the dollar he borrowed earlier in the day.

When you hang out with homeless people there is never a shortage of drama. As the night got crazier, Adriana reappeared and was yelling at Eric while she held a metal pipe in her hand, telling Eric to shut his mouth or she was going to hit him with the pipe. At this point, Eric was wearing a blue bandana and a pair of pants. Mary reminded me that Eric was also part of the "Bloods" gang. I told Mary that Eric just had swollen pride and was talking from two sides of his mouth, and that he was no gang member. Bloods do not wear blue bandanas, so the theory behind Eric's being in a gang was squashed again. I have read a lot about people saying that there are gangs on Venice Beach. Believe me, if there are gangs here, I never saw any members in groups, and I know this beach like the back of my hand, having traveled it day and night. The police do a great job on this beach and never once did I run into a gang member, not even late at night. I know a former gang member from the beach, but after doing time in prison he is now reformed. Even he told me that the gang members cover a 32 block radius near downtown LA.

Mary was funny. As Mary yelled at a man walking by whom she called another "Manson disciple," she told Jane and me, "We have nothing to worry about, we have our Japanese bodyguard." I asked Mary, "Who is your bodyguard?" Mary said, "Ho Chi Minh Trail, Kazuo." Then I said, "Why is Kazuo your bodyguard, is he tough?" "cause he's Japanese, so automatically he can defend himself," she said. Kazuo slept in a tiny area underneath the cement walk that leads halfway to the beach.

After stereotyping Kazuo, Mary was telling us her perspective on different races. She said, "My Sicilian friend Tony. You want to write a whole book of crap about homelessness in Venice, talk to that fool over there." I called her a racist because she has a negative stereotype about every race.

One thing I will say about Kazuo is that he is unlike any homeless person I met. Unlike Mary, if he borrowed a quarter, the quarter was paid back by the end of the day. One morning I treated him to breakfast that was $5.50. That night he paid back the breakfast loan. Regardless of whether or not he was homeless, Kazuo had great pride and never wanted to owe anyone anything. This tells me a great deal about his character. For a homeless person to chase me down to pay back a quarter, it tells me that as a Japanese national he feels that honesty carries over from his culture. This is part of the Japanese social model that values ethics, instilled at a young age and carried over into his adult character. Even the homeless have pride. I have friends who owe me money for twenty years who have never paid me back.

In the late 1990s an acquaintance of ours came from Japan and took a taxicab ride from John F. Kennedy Airport to Long Island, which is roughly a $50 cab ride. When the cab driver realized that the Japanese man did not speak any English, the "ugly American" realized he could cash in on the man. The Japanese man had no concept of the American dollar, and as a result, he was taken for $500 by the cab driver for a twenty-five minute ride. I was outraged by this! It is the reason that people around the world dislike us. One bad act can negatively label a population. Perception counts!

Mary had been to Social Services earlier in the day, where she received a check for $355 for motel expenses to stay for two weeks on "Skid Row," in the bad part of LA. She said she would try to sell it and collect the money, but she ended up losing the voucher because she did not use it by the instructed date. She then told us that she lost much of her food-assistance privileges because she tried to sell marijuana to an undercover police officer, which I already knew from her records. This mistake cost her! She said she used to receive $210 dollars for food stamps for the entire month; now she receives nothing.

Trying to teach a person to make better choices is very hard. Take Joel for example; we see that he is at the age where he feels there is hope and a future. Then we see Mary who is drowned with the anguish and choices she has made, which have left her in a chronic state of homelessness for twenty years, making poor choice after poor choice.

The homeless people I met live for today; they do not worry about tomorrow or the future. The assumption from the government is that if a person is making money from selling drugs, then he or she does not need government assistance to buy food. As a taxpayer, I can totally understand the government's logic.

Mary then began to tell me about her alcoholism, something she never would have told me when I first met her back when she threatened to kill me. She said she could not buy booze around here because she had been banned from all of the establishments on/or near the beach, so she was forced to walk to Santa Monica to buy her liquor.

She said the main reason she drinks is to hide her pain, a consistent theme throughout the time we spent with Mary. Mary said, "I go get me a half a pint of vodka in Santa Monica and then I don't open it until I get back to Venice. I cannot drink it in Santa Monica because they will arrest you and put you in jail in the drunk-tank even if it is your first fucking drink. I have a few injuries and I am in pain and I don't want to think about the pain and I don't want to start shooting heroin for the pain, so the vodka will relax me, make me happy, and it will clear up my chapped lips and make my mouth feel better... [laughing] like mouthwash, and then when the bottle's empty, I'll be sleeping somewhere, and God will watch out for me." To conclude her story, Mary then began singing a Kenny Rogers song, "The Gambler": "You gotta know when to hold 'em, know when to fold 'em, know when to walk away and when to run. You never count your money when you are sittin' at the table. There'll be time enough for countin', when the dealin's done." This seemed to sum up her philosophy on life.

As we sat on our bench, many tourists passed by, probably wondering why we would sit here talking to homeless people. Mary grows on a person, and after a while, like Mary, I can say that many of the homeless people became our friends on an interpersonal and conversational level. Even the LAPD police cruiser slowed by the walk several times, looking at the way we were dressed versus the attire of the homeless. They stared at us, but they asked us nothing. They knew Mary well and they stopped and called her over to the patrol car to chat with her. The funniest part about this is she was wearing a "Support the LAPD" hat. Imagine, she is arrested almost two hundred times and yet, she has the nerve to wear this hat? Mary gives Venice Beach residents the colorful and mystical appeal they have.

 **Chapter 32**

LA County Jail

Photo: Jane A. Lackner
Mary, wearing O'Connell's clothes before we talked the LAPD out of arresting her only to be arrested this evening anyway.

Back to Mary.

It had been more than a week since we last saw Mary. After asking many of my contacts, I finally found out that she was back in the county jail. Apparently, she violated her parole by not showing up to meet with her parole officer. Damn Mary! The law is strict and when a person breaks the law, there are consequences. I was worried about Mary. I then referred back to my reporter days and decided to investigate by first calling the prison system, but they did not have a record of her on file.

In developing a few police sources while here over the last two nights we discovered quite a bit of information, which we previously did not have. Even with Mary's full name and maiden name, I could not track her down. I found out that she had called a mutual friend, and I learned where she was days before the police told us what had happened to her.

By now readers know that Mary is not a stranger to the prison system as her sixteen-page record indicated. The police we stopped one night who knows Mary said that she beat a long stay in prison, and another source in the police department told us she served four years in addition to the most recent nine-month stay. They wouldn't tell us what crime she committed to get the lengthy time in prison, but her record has so many charges that the long stay may have been in Texas, her previous residents. Mary denied that she spent four years in the system. At age fifty-four, she cannot afford to go back to the big house at this point in her life.

One of the last conversations we had with Mary was about how people treat her. She said, "Professor, do you know I have been raped, robbed, beat up, and nobody [Mary is crying] has ever been prosecuted for hurting me, Bo."

Mary has had many a tough day. First off, she is ill. She had her breast removed while in prison over the last nine months due to breast cancer, and now she has a huge bulge in her stomach from her hernia. The situation seems hopeless and seriously a heartbreak. She claims she has not received any type of chemotherapy or radiation for the breast cancer. She says she refuses to be a guinea pig.

A few weeks went by until finally we ran into Mary's friend Mary's friend Amore, and she told us she saw Mary and that her homeless family was looking for her. Perception: we go from being Jane, the English Teacher, and Bo the Communication Professor to being perceived as Mary's homeless family. As we walked up the walk toward the Venice Pier, mystically, there was Mary walking with a basket of belongings as she talked with two very nice young men, one from Los Angeles and one from Texas. We missed her very much, her laugh, her goodness, her lashing out against society, and her smile. Then a vendor who knew Mary walked by and said something to her. Mary had a forty-ounce bottle of beer in her hand, which she threw at the vendor, missing his head by inches as the glass bottle broke all over the walk. I could have cried. Going back to what I said earlier in the book, people in this neighborhood take care of their own problems. A few of the homeless yelled at Mary, then they all cleaned up the mess she made with the bottle and went their own way. The night with a full moon went on and we stayed out until after midnight talking to Mary, Adriana, and Brittany who was back on our bench in the usual spot.

In this environment, once again when I think of Mary, her tragedy is the most profound. I realize that her life was robbed from her in many ways even in her early childhood with a father who is a Vietnam Veteran, and a broken home which lacked guidance. She never had a support system during the loss of the love and spirit of her son. This profoundly affected her life causing her to numb her pain and reality by drinking alcohol. Deep down, we know Mary is only harming herself. We know that deep inside, underneath the anguish that she lives with everyday, she has so much love and true friendship to give. But she also fights behind a system that fails her. Mary is not solely responsible for her actions. She is plagued by mental health issues and she suffers with deep guilt and depression as the leading cause of her behavior. When she takes her medications and isn't drinking, Mary is functional, polite, doesn't even curse, and she can hold a terrific intelligent conversation. Putting her back in jail is not a solution to her problems, but it does keep her safe. Perhaps putting her in a detoxification unit for a longer period of time will increase her chances of survival as she learns to take on greater responsibility for her life so that in return she makes better choices which keep her alive and out of trouble.

The system succeeded by placing Mary in the proper mental health authority's hands and into a rehabilitative system. She was attending Alcoholics Anonymous meetings six hours a day and she was clean for more than forty days. It is cheaper to attend an AA meeting than to house a prisoner in a correctional facility.

Mary needs AA to get her life back on track. Maybe it will work for her and enable her to make positive choices that keep her spirit alive and improve her desire to live. As long as she doesn't hurt anyone or herself why cant the system press and order Mary to continue attending?

Mary lives life on a rollercoaster on a ride to nowhere in and out of prison so many times, I lost track. She met a local man she has known for years named Bud. Bud opened his door and heart to her. I got the sense that Mary was going to make a last attempt to redeem her life. After we left Venice Beach for the final book tour, Mary was released from prison and she found hope with Bud.

Bud and I spoke numerous times by telephone. He was a solid, stable and reliable retired blue collar guy. Bud, 73 years old, told me he loved Mary. He provided temporary shelter for her and took her into his home until she could get back on her feet. She never drank in his presence and proved clean while living in his home. He told me that Mary's friends on Venice Beach are not truly her friends. The friends she has are few and far between. Diane, her husband Abraham, Shyla, the Captain of Venice, and David who owns the corner store, care very much about Mary. I have witnessed other homeless people though, mooch off what little Mary receives from the system who know how to play the system so that they satisfy their addictions. They will take whatever little income social services give Mary when they are with her. Mary was happy and sober the last five times I talked to her by phone from Bud's house. I even introduced her to my class when we discussed non-verbal behaviors from a homeless person's perspective. Each day, I cry deep down for her, praying, hoping, that Mary finds peace and happiness for the rest of her life.

Sadly, for Mary though, a new tragedy fills her life. One of her only caring human shields of protection and guardian angels died out. In May, I had just finished teaching my classes for the semester when my phone rang. It was Mary. She was very upset and I could hear the quiver in her voice as I asked her to stay calm and tell me what happened. She said, "Bud was supposed to have an operation, but it was postponed." I said okay. She said, "Bud died." My heart just hit the floor. I asked God, what more obstacles does this woman have to face in her life?

The night Bud died, Mary said that she said goodnight to Bud at around eight o'clock when she stayed up to watch the news. The next morning she went into the other room to say good morning to her friend, but he didn't respond and was still and not breathing.

While Bud was lying dead in his bed, I told Mary to be sure she did not leave the house or the police may accuse her of wrong doing with her record. After hearing the obvious pain in her voice, I really did not know what to say to comfort her, but I knew that this whole incident might throw Mary off the deep end and keep her deep in the woods. Finally, after more than four hours of waiting, the Los Angeles County Coroner arrived to take Bud away.

Since Bud's death, Mary was again homeless and back on the streets of Venice Beach and Los Angeles, the very streets which has taken her life apart.

We cannot change the situation with Bud. In trying to bring about awareness and positive change, the homeless themselves have to want to change. Like Mary, many get so stuck in this lifestyle that it becomes a bigger part of a person's psyche and eventually consumes their self concept with such denial that they don't care what people think. It is a Darwinism at work and the theory that the strong survive brings to light the way the homeless live, like Nomads. Most feel like there is no hope, but hope comes to those who are inspired to change too. Be it by choice or not, as long as a person is responsible, treats others with respect and cares about our environment then people will better understand the issue. The problem is there is the criminal element of homeless who are in and out of jail who become homeless only to land back in jail after beating the public. It bugs me! This is where government needs to make the biggest change, in serving us with the option for consequences against those who continue to commit violent acts against the public only to be rewarded with release from prison due to overcrowded jails. On the flipside of the negative effects, there has been success in transforming people with criminal behavior into becoming productive citizens, but not all will follow a positive transformation.

In 2004, President Bush announced his "Prisoner Re-Entry Initiative (PRI) designed to assist ex-prisoners and the communities to which they return." Through this program, returning offenders are linked to faith-based and community institutions that help ex-prisoners find work and avoid a relapse into a life of criminal activity. I actually know one such Venice Beach man who has a college degree in Business Administration from the University of Southern California who has made a complete transformation, but this program grew out of the U.S. Department of Labor's "Ready4work" program.

A nearby shelter in Venice Beach called St. Joseph's frequently helps homeless people to do the same thing. We should do the same for the homeless who are willing and able where mentoring, employment and other transitional services are provided to thousands of homeless ex-inmates.

As of November 9, 2007, "10,361 PRI participants have been enrolled in the Ready4work program and 6,035 participants have been placed into jobs. That strategic direction equals success. PRI participants' one-year post-release recidivism rate is currently less than half the national average recidivism rate" (U.S. Department of Labor, 2008).

In another success story about the system, last November 2007, the White House hosted the first Prisoner Reentry Summit in Los Angeles, CA. More than 1,000 representatives from non-profit community organizations gathered for two days of training and workshops, joining leaders from both the private and public sectors. They include, White House Faith Based Community Institutions Director, Jay Hein and Secretary of Labor, Elaine Chao. Highlighting the key role of FBCOs in helping ex-inmates to build successful lives, Chao said, "We know that the long-term financial costs of re-incarceration far exceed the cost of reentry programs" (Whitehouse.Gov, 2008). This is the same type of work program we have to create on a national scale for the able and willing homeless in finding solutions. By reaching out to the most needy we can change people's lives and better them. The heaviest cost and most important reason is the loss of human dignity when people are living lives of poverty, addiction, and despair. We can break this cycle through hard work and professional people.

Tracking performance can facilitate positive changes if the right personnel are in place doing the tracking. People who have the ability to be the watchdogs for the taxpayers and people who can pressure able bodied homeless people to get back to work, meet the demands of an already confused society, and win back their lives will only come upon the willing and acceptable homeless. With the proper intervention Mary, a habitual 5150 can change, but the question is, is she worth the system's investment? It cost more to house her than it does to treat her.

Mary's way to better her life was short lived, and the fact remains, when she is not drinking she maintains as normal a life possible for a person with her background.

Early in June 2008, nearly three years after meeting her, Mary called me very excited that I was visiting Venice Beach. I told her to stay out of trouble. I suppose the pain of losing Bud was too much and a week later I watched Mary, of all places, on June 16, 2008, on You-Tube where she had her pants down in the middle of Main Street in Venice while she squatted down, drunk, and helpless. Again, Mary was the victim of someone's laugh as a man filmed the entire pitiful episode of Mary crossing the street, being made a victim of her own victimization as she washes away more pain induced by alcohol and life. Mary looked frail weak, pitiful, depressed and beaten down by life as she is yet again, headed back to a jail cell in the woman's jail at Lynwood Correctional Facility. I came to the conclusion and realization that as hard as I tried to help her change, I failed because she failed. We all fail because we keep feeding a broken down system which has good intentions, but it has never fully been held accountable state which carefully tracks people who fail the system with what the system provides.

Mary's friend Marty who allowed Mary to live in his home a few years ago even tried to offer me a deal that I could use his car on the condition that I visit Mary at Lynwood, but knowing her emotion, I felt it best for Mary to remain sober and less emotional, only it should be in AA and not jail. I did leave a message for Mary's parole officer to get a better understanding of how much time she will be incarcerated for. It is easy to predict that with all the pain in her life and how she handles it, it was only a matter of time that she would be right back on the streets drinking, finding trouble, and even risking her life to possibly be killed.

Throughout the course of this book, Mary is the one person who provides insight into the people who are homeless and some reasons why people are homelessness. I couldn't visit her in Lynwood Correctional Facility this time because I felt that it may bring her more emotional pain than good. It is also a way to send Mary a subtle but honest message her choices landed her where she is and ruined the opportunity to see people who genuinely care about her.

Mary's life is based on death. We all have something, someone to answer to.

I close this chapter on Mary's life with the following excerpt of a letter sent to me from Mary, who wrote this letter from the same jail as Paris Hilton, who received national media publicity on a daily basis from Los Angeles. Mary again landed herself back in prison, a cycle which owns her. Mary now finds herself in a life filled with trouble, pain, and suffering, blaming herself for her child's death.

As fate would have it, this letter is dated July 20, 2007, a year to the day since Coby was murdered. Mary writes from a prison cell.

Dear Shyla, Bo & Jane,

They got me for absconding that means not reporting (to my Parole Officer). Well, I reported once, but not to the new parole agent. Since I am on high-control, they have to be able to visit me once a month as well as me visiting their office. I had been going to my case manager Olga, who is trying to find me a motel for a two-week voucher in a neighborhood that is not too bad. She said if I have any problems with my parole officer, I should contact her. I do not know the number, but if someone would contact her so she can contact him, perhaps I can get out of here, otherwise I will be having a hearing 13 business days from now. I am sorry everyone. Ya'll were all trying to help me and I appreciate it very much. If you can visit, it would be nice to see you here at "Paris" jail. Write soon, love to all, Love Mary

Chapter 33

Hail to the Chief

Photo: William G. O'Connell
The Chief sprinkles his spirit before the Venice Drum Circle kicks off its weekly ritual.

Venice Beach is one of the only places that I know of in America where people claim self-ownership of land. Most people would be hard pressed to believe this next man's story. He is probably one of the most interesting, daring, and intelligent characters in the book. He may also be the one person who has the vision for change, and the perfect person to speak to the entire community, filled with activists and politicians so that we can figure out a way to fix the homeless problem. Chief Keetoowah or "Chief" is what most of the young people call him, and so did I. The Chief is an amazing person who twenty-five years ago ended up on the beach in Carmel, which is in Northern California. That path took him here to Venice Beach where on a daily basis the Chief guides, directs, and produces a quality of life unlike any other.

I asked the Chief why he is homeless and he said, "I lost the world I thought I lived in, the world I thought I cared for. I was in my early thirties and finally growing up. Soon after I came to Venice Beach, doing what I came here on earth to do: holding back the hate." The Chief, a Native American, said that he would always be a political activist. He is also German, Spanish, and French. He said, "In my life as a political and environmental activist, I have talked to many of society's supposed leaders and they all have the same idea, peace, but they are not living the idea. I have moved on to something greater here on Venice Beach, and this land and beach belong to the people."

The Chief talked to us for forty-five minutes as he waved his flag that has a picture of the American bald eagle, our national symbol. He also carries a genuine badge, which reads "Universal Protection Officer, Omega Sector," attached to his flagpole. The badge symbolizes his tradition as an environmental activist.

249

We wanted to hear more of what the Chief had to say so I arranged to meet him on his turf, the world-famous "Venice Drum Circle," two weeks later. In fact, we were clinging to his every word. The Chief has an aura about him. There was something uniquely different about the Chief in comparison to the other homeless people we met. I made the decision to use the Chief for the front cover of this book because I felt his spirit and pride represented the way homeless people in general ride the spirit of America, with pride, regardless of their personal constitutions.

Everybody here has a story. The Chief is on YouTube in a 2:54-long piece where the Chief is at work waving his flag and doing his dance, once in the beginning of the video and then in the last few minutes of the video. There were countless times during the course of writing this book that I thought about my students' lives and some of the issues they have and the hard lives they live. The Chief's spirit reminded me of one of two of my former students Zeshan, who lost his brother on 911 in the World Trade Center attacks, and shortly after, he lost his father, and Logan Sappell, who has this positive aura about her. Like my son, both Zeshan and Logan are heroes to me. They have overcome many of life's most daunting obstacles finding a centering force which drives their self-hero. They have endured, which propels them in a positive way.

A student visiting California during our stay actually showed up at my apartment with his friends. James Kim is one of the most likeable young students I have taught. James said that Venice is fascinating and that he wished his trip was longer. I told James to go to the drum circle to meet the Chief, but I cautioned James and his friends about the dangers as they walked the beach. James is a person who believes in change. Change for a better world through peace and love. He cares about education and about people.

Upon my visit with the Chief, he explained that he has been a political activist for more than twenty years. He said he is fifty-eight years old and he told us that there are two sides to the beach and that nature's side is west, the Pacific Ocean, but on this side of the beach is the different class of homeless people whom he calls "refugees." I never quite thought of the homeless as refugees, but I thought the term was appropriate. The Chief said that on this beach there are the children, whom we protect. Then he said the women are stronger because they are the source of life, and all life comes from them, so we have to respect them as the source of life. He also said that we are all homeless the minute we leave the mother's womb. He declared, "The men have to be strong, but those who are weak need our help; the lovers are the strong. Our mission here is to be free and love everyone. We are not afraid of the "haters" or the people who are here to harm us."

In fact, he said, he will go right up to a gang member with a gun and risk being killed to stand up for peace. It is this mentality that is intriguing about the Chief. He is a man with a defined purpose, a purpose which by the average person's standards defies our reason for existence. Yet, living in the material world shelters us in a way from the essence of life doesn't it?

In one of the most compelling stories of how people feel about homelessness around the country, eleven year old Brenden Foster of Bothell, Wash., who was given that prognosis earlier this year after learning he was suffering from leukemia last December, the answer was probably not what you'd expect. "I was coming back from one of my clinic appointments and I saw this big thing of homeless people and then I thought I should just get them something," Foster said. Instead of asking for an expensive toy or a fancy vacation, he decided to focus all his remaining energy on feeding the homeless. "They're probably starving, so give them a chance," he said. After inspiring a national food drive, a week later Foster passed away from this devastating illness. This thankless good deed of giving is something the Chief could align with because he is selfless. Brenden Foster left behind his "self-hero" legacy by helping the homeless on his dying bed.

To give up opportunity and everything the world offers for the Chief's current state is a fascinating revelation defining his purpose.

The Chief went on to tell us stories about Einstein, to understanding the nuclear physicist's view of jet propulsion and speech-writing, right down to the political vision of the country. I must say, the Chief's ideology had a thought-provoking aspect to it and he is very popular on Venice Beach. He said, "I personally as being a citizen of the world believe that until the 'controllers' recognize the changes we need there will not be world peace."

The Chief said that the biggest war is famine around the world. He said about famine, "It hurts me. When I wake up every day, I save my energy for the community, for the children and the people." The minute he left us after talking about his life, at least ten younger people gathered around him to talk to and listen to him. It was as if he was a father figure to these teenagers. Amazing!

The Chief calls the homeless youngsters his children and the homeless his tribe. In my professional opinion, the Chief is a legitimate advocate for peace, love, and respect for human life. He substitutes society's philosophy with his philosophy on unconditional love.

A few weeks later on July 29, I again joined the Chief in the Venice Beach Drum Circle, but beforehand, I interviewed the Chief in one of my most memorable interviews. The Chief is a descendent of the traditional Cherokee tribe. That tribal philosophy is one he has been instilling in the young homeless people who live here on the beach for the past five years. With his education, he knows the psychology of simplicity in reaching the masses of lovers, haters, victims, victimizers, and nearly everyone who is homeless on this beach.

The Chief said that his tribal name is Keetoowah, which in the Cherokee Nation means "the principal people," and in the Blackfoot Nation it means "the real people." The Keetoowah or United Keetoowah Band of Cherokee has been around for 179 years since the

Keetoowah relocated to Tahlequah from Arkansas after signing the Treaty of 1828. "I study what the sound sounds like and then I say, that's what my name is. That is the name of my colony, so that is who I shall be. Why should I be anything less than that? If I am, then guess what? Then I am living a lie," the Chief said.

Living homeless for more than twenty years has given the Chief the opportunity to reflect on life at the deepest levels. He is no stranger to education. In fact, the Chief said that the age of five, he advanced to the second grade as a gifted student. As an adult, he worked his way through UCLA and Pasadena City College, and was hired by NASA's Jet Propulsion Laboratory at California Institute of Technology in Pasadena, where he received his PhD in Nuclear Astrophysics. He also said that he worked for the unmanned space station for NASA. I took the liberty to call NASA in Pasadena; the Division of Records informed me when I gave the Chief's legal name for verification that while the Chief worked at NASA he may have received top-secret clearance, and all they could give me was a yes or no to verify his story. They did not deny that he worked there, and the Chief's story adds to his credibility.

The biggest question is why is the Chief homeless?

It is not as complicated as I thought it would be to understand why the Chief lives this unconventional lifestyle if you are from the generation of important events of the 1960s. Three of the most influential movements in US history were in the 1960s: the radical, defining

Vietnam antiwar, civil rights, and Black Power movements that changed and shaped the history of this country for future generations. Through these movements, a person's status in this country meant that he or she had a stake in the future of America as equal rights became an expression valued by mainstream society. People earned something Americans feel. The Chief played a peaceful role in the movement for peace, as his *modus operandi* is peace-driven.

The antiwar movement "happened during a time of unprecedented student activism reinforced in numbers by the demographically significant baby boomers, but grew to include a wide and varied cross-section of Americans from all walks of life." The "opposition to the war grew as television and press coverage graphically showed the suffering of both civilians and conscripts. In 1965, demonstrations in New York City attracted 25,000 marchers; within two years similar demonstrations drew several hundred thousand participants in Washington, D.C., London, and other European capitals. Most of the demonstrations were peaceful, though acts of civil disobedience—intended to provoke arrest—were common" (Answers.com, 2008).

One of the greatest peace leaders of our time was Dr. Martin Luther King Jr., who represented oppressed people in America during the Civil Rights Movement. His message of injustice propelled a larger peace movement. In a sense, MLK gave America a wakeup call that led to further movements, creating future generations of spokespeople involved in movements for change. He did this by building relationships between activists and politicians to balance the power in favor of the people of this country. Terms like "the counterculture," "hippie movement," "flower children," and the "sit-in movement," which was "a series of peaceful protests that brought renewed national attention to the injustices of the segregated South and eventually forced the federal government to protect the rights of African-Americans actively." The Chief taught me valuable lessons on counterculture which "a term that describes rules, norms, social behavior of a cultural group or sub-culture, that run counter to mainstream society equivalent to political opposition.

The Black Power movement, which was another political movement that arose in the mid-1960s, "strove to express a new racial consciousness among Blacks in the United States which represented racial dignity and self-reliance (i.e. freedom from white authority in both economic and political arenas). To others, it was economic in orientation" (Esec-Nuno-Alveres, 2008). The Black Panthers also evolved from this movement of radical change in treatment of a people.

All of the movements of the 1960s have our younger generation asking many questions as students are being taught in both high school and college classrooms around the country about the study of US policy and social thought.

The Chief recalled all of the movements of the 1960s as he provided a clear and articulate recap of all the biographies of leaders and artists he has studied. He has made it his interest to study the works of

Albert Einstein, Dante Alighieri, Mahatma Gandhi, John F. Kennedy, Harry S. Truman, John Dewey, Dr. Martin Luther King Jr., Pablo Picasso, Vincent van Gogh, Abraham Lincoln, and George Washington.

As a former national speech judge, having listened to countless informative and persuasive speeches over the past five years, I can tell that the Chief is a master public speaker. It is hard to believe that with his education, he has been out of the work environment for decades. Regardless, he has not lost his edge on what makes the world tick. He is the greatest hope for the homeless who need a voice of reason.

Venice is a sanctuary, "some place like a Mecca, like a church, like a paradise, a heaven on earth where people come from all over the world, 205 nations, and as they look out to the ocean, look out to the sky, and say, you know what I feel, a sense of peace here, calm, love, unconditional love, agape love," proclaimed the Chief.

On the question of how the Chief views the young people today, he said, "The young people of today have not been given the opportunity that I had when I was growing up. Many have no heroes. Many have no man or woman on this planet that they can look up to, not a mother or a father, cousin or nieces or nephews, or anyone. No aunts and uncles...no one to look up to give them the answers, to where do you find peace in your mind and in your hearts?"

Most young people may say they find peace in using drugs and alcohol, but the Chief says, "Shame on them, because it is not fair. See where it is? It is in their own hearts, their healers are in their own hearts," he said, referring to some of the young recording artists whom our young people look up to. He went on to say that the heroes are there, but you have to go looking for them.

The Chief said, "I beg to differ with a lot of adults today, especially the elders like my age who come from the movement. They call them 'trash children' today, or the 'throwaway generation.'"

The Chief has also set up his own negotiating table when there is trouble between young people on the beach, and the young people know to come to him when problems escalate, as they are encouraged by other "Chief tribal members" to talk to the Chief. Basically, I met "the man" who paves the way for the underground homeless. He is revered by the younger homeless because he is rational in his quest to free the mind from cultural materialism and consumerism, the very proponent of society which causes so many ethical self-induced problems.

Why can't the police or even our government communicate like the Chief? I thought. He said he tells the young homeless people on Venice, "If you have a problem, you come to the Chief. We will sit down and have negotiations and dialogue to discuss the matter, what is at issue? You got hate, come on, I am going to give you a dose of love. So that's what I have done." In one word, I found the best way to define the Chief: "respect." In a nomad sense, the Chief said that he helps young people based on spirituality and the positive mentors he has had over the years. The man knows how to engage people.

Being connected to love rather than hate takes a big person; it also makes logical sense. The Chief said, "I got connected with giving love from all humanity in my life, American, black, white, striped, pink, and colorless. It did not make a difference; human beings in this country brought me up. They said, 'Go to school.' They paid for the school." He said that in sending him to school, the American people showed belief and faith in him as a good seed. We would be hypocrites to judge because the Chief did with his education what he believes he was guided to do by a higher power. How can we in good moral consciousness disagree with his homeless lifestyle? Wasn't Jesus homeless? The Chief has taken nature and thrown out materialism as an ideal as he lives what he feels is a justified existence.

The Chief said, "I was going to be someone who would pass on what heroism is about, what sacrifice is about, and what unconditional agape love is about, and these children see it in me because they watch everything I do in the sand. I live a nomadic life, I tell everyone, 'No, I don't have all the answers,' but when I see the evil wicked ones, I tell the 'tribal members' to tell the haters" to not go down the road of hate and destruction that causes fights within the circle of the homeless here on the beach. The Chief said, "Hate gets you nowhere and love conquers all."

Before hitting the drum circle where the thumping vibration can be moving, I asked the Chief what entering the circle means to him. He said, "It's gorgeous. Let me say that it is beyond exquisite, but on the spiritual end, I say I think the creator, my creator, okay, all these people from around the world, 205 nations, playing drums from the youngest, which is less than eighteen months old, all the way up to 108 years old. We are all from different cultures, different backgrounds, different religious persuasions, a variety of people, some rich, some poor, and we are all intermingling with a sound. With a sound of what, with a sound of a drum."

Since we could hear the loud banging of one of the largest crowds of people I have ever seen gathered on the beach, I asked the Chief where the instrument, the drum, comes from. With the beat of hundreds, and even more than a thousand people gathering in the drum circle thirty yards from where we were standing, the Chief said, "I went back, did some research and a study in a narrative, and found out that the drum was started in this hemisphere forty-five thousand years ago. So I went back forty-five thousand years and I tried to imagine myself as sort of Neanderthal or tribal person that did not want anything to do with technology. I wanted to find the true essence of what makes people truly be happy. When I found this drum circle was making people happy, I realized it's the center point of my chiefdom and I won't allow anything on this planet to disturb this drum circle."

Playing devil's advocate, I asked the Chief a thought-provoking question about what a naysayer might say about him, looking at him for the first time when he or she might have a different perception of him. I even went so far as to ask the Chief how he would respond to someone calling him fake. The Chief smiled and peacefully said, "Let me put it to you like this. My heart is pure, and my mind is clear. Over the last forty-five years of my life, I have seen and heard and read, and done research, analysis, and I found out what kind of person I am deep down in the heart. You see, there is nothing really on a planet that a man or a woman has or possess that I want or desire. The only thing I look for is peace." He ended by asking me a question: "How do you keep peace?" I said to him, "I am looking peace square in the eyes, man to man, human to human, and I am seeing peace on earth for the first time in a long time." The Chief taught me a lesson on peace, which I would again like to quote. He said, "Every driving force that I've seen against peace has folded. I have my view of what peace is. If I could expound by action, word, or deed, by just being myself, being real, being a principled person, and being a chosen person, then that's what I will do because, see, that is what everyone looks for. Everyone looks for their self-hero, and I say to myself, Wow, I have my self-heroship and people give me the human and unconditional love that I have always desired." The Chief went on to say, "So, wait a minute, I am almost sixty years old now. I have been looking for something all my life that was already there. It was invisible, but now that it has been shown to me, I will let you know it. Love first, and peace will follow. Now if I throw out the low-capsule formula first, peace will follow, with positive joyfulness, positive expounding of that, all of the sudden we have what we call 'a movement,' the love movement, the unconditional human love movement."

This is a man whom I would love to have as a guest speaker in my classroom. The younger people adore him.

Joining a drum circle is an awesome experience on Venice Beach. The drum circle invites hundreds, even thousands of people from every lifestyle into one big circle, with the different types of drums beating felt like a pow-wow of sorts. The Chief said, "People used to call it the drug circle, the scum circle, and I beg to differ. I was the throwaway generation circle, so I beg to differ."

The Chief talked about labels and said, "What gives anyone the right to say who these people are? They don't know that person, so what do I do, they have to put labels on them. So I say this is a free zone, you have no labels, you belong to no one. Like the spirit says, we are mounting our wings and say thank you for the opportunity to be representative of the human spirit. For two years I have been fortunate to work with this circle; miracles are happening! Last week a young father held his two-week-old baby inside the circle!"

Everyone holding down this circle just keeps coming with love and the beat. It is one of the largest circles of free expression and all are welcome with no discrimination: black, white, Hispanic, European, Asian, red, gay, straight, men, women, young, old, secure, insecure, mentally ill, alcoholic, drug user, small, or large.

I lived in the moment as the FREE sounding beat of hundreds of drums and smiles rallied in support of the inspiration of the circle, while the Chief of Venice waved his flag with the bald eagle, and the American Flag planted dead in the middle of the circle! What a sight! Peace to the drum circle and a truly positive experience.

Putting into perspective life on Venice Beach and the Chief's opportunity to make a difference, we bowed to each other with a traditional Native American arm shake, not handshake, and we then grabbed elbows and touched heads. Now that was an experience I had never had before in my life. The love of nature at work through people like the Chief made me feel like writing this book was worth every minute of the exhausting days and nights I have spent with the homeless. The Chief left NASA as a Nuclear Astrophysicist in his twenties because the government was fueling nuclear rockets to outer space. What if one exploded? I don't believe I would be writing this book.

Hail to the Chief for providing me with one of the most educational intercultural experience as a world traveler that I have ever experienced!

EPILOGUE

Chapter 34

"Reflections on the Endless Summer"

Photo: William G. O'Connell
Jane after a hard day's work ready to go to dinner.

As the sunny and beautiful endless summer comes to a close, I walked over to a local long haired Spanish man named Glenn who I met a week earlier on the beach who was finishing his vacation and getting ready to go back to the culinary trade school he is attending in

Los Angeles. We discussed how awesome Venice Beach can be. It also reminded me of a conversation I had with Jane earlier in the day when she related that she did not feel the same about Venice as the first time we visited. While we both enjoyed the beach, the one thing missing from this final trip was Mary who is back in prison. We both missed our friend even though we enjoyed the beach each day. Instead of enjoying Mary's company in the evening, we were subjected to behaviors that went beyond the realm of abnormality we had already experienced. Jane was more uncomfortable than I was with this new group of homeless inhabitants of Venice Beach.

Looking down at the sand, I walk into the edge of the Pacific Ocean, waves crashing as I watched a piece of driftwood in the waves find a destiny of its own. The smell of Venice Beach's salty air has me thinking about all of the people we met on this journey. The beauty of the ocean, the school of peaceful, playful dolphin breeching the water, and the sound of children running circles in and out of the beach sand and ocean is tranquil, especially while a homeless man combs the beach. It is the last full day to the end of this year's journey and I can't help but think how I have changed since living in Venice Beach each summer. The three or more years I have spent writing this book building relationships that to the average person may seem meaningless, has become very real for me. It has allowed me to appreciate what I have, what I don't have, and how fast life changes. In a way it has helped me to shape my future because through this experience I can better understand an international crisis and place my finger on the pulse of what makes this unpopular segment of society tick.

When we first arrived at Venice Beach, we had a simple taste of paradise, and we misjudged many of the homeless people we met, but after we spent a little time here, we discovered more that homelessness affects us all.

In a democratic sense, don't we as a nation enable and disable people? Personally I know that sometimes I can get wrapped up in my own life, but in truth, I do want to aid in finding solutions to this problem.

Prevention and foresight of homelessness is the key to changing the outcome of this dilemma, but it will take perseverance and responsibility from every aspect of society. From educators, parents, social workers, and government to the homeless themselves, the only way we can better manage this crisis is to begin to identify the "at risk" homeless and create international awareness at the highest, most powerful levels so that we can change this epidemic.

If we do not care enough to understand their problems, we invite a greater problem because the homeless will continue to leave their mark on our communities while our children look on. Perhaps our new President elect Barack Obama will provide hope for homeless children. My hope is that maybe with books like this, we will help to enlighten the public about this unpopular segment of our population, increase public awareness, identify the causes and effects, and finally, find possible solutions for homelessness.

Maybe stronger guidance, more love, or a better family life could have taken someone from the ruthless grip society has on our homeless, and instead lead a troubled person in the right direction. We have to find a way for the homeless to cooperate with people who are willing to change this problem so that they feel they can trust the guide.

It's easy to conclude that many of the homeless we met made poor life choices, are victims of circumstance, or both. I pose many questions.

Imagine being drafted to fight for your country at eighteen then suffering the cause and effects of post traumatic stress disorder? Wars tear lives apart. Sometimes people can not muster up the strength to be more productive as a citizen. For Pruitt, it wasn't his plan in life to be a soldier, yet he took the cards he was dealt and made the best of it. We never saw Pruitt again. It is unimaginable to most of us to grasp the concept of not having a place to sleep or wondering where your next meal will come from.

Imagine being mentally ill, depressed, bi-polar, or helpless only to find yourself later in life like Yvonne, Va, Julie, and Jason who is unable to wash away the mental suffering they face each day because they do not know how, they are helpless. Imagine if your child became involved with drugs, got strung out with no one to turn to and nowhere to go with no options left when we as parents leave this earth. What would you do to prevent the unknown?

Take Adriana and Brittney, Jessie, Tracy, and Steve the "Venice Queen." Based on their lifestyles, they may very well remain in their state of homelessness as the vicious and ruthless cycle winds like a black hole to nowhere.

Imagine having no options in life after living a productive life, losing everything you have? It is not impossible. It is hard to predict the future, but the troubled economy is quickly painting a dismal picture for the once stable American family's future. Hundreds of thousands of people have lost their jobs, their homes, and face a major crisis.

In September, 2008 the Dow plunged an all-time record 700 and 800 points on Wall Street for the second time in a month. Many economists predict the worse.

Almost all of the homeless we met were from broken homes. Then there were other homeless like Charlie who came from a privileged home where his parents were successful financially. But like any other American family, dealing with the tragedy of drug, alcohol abuse, and other addictions can ultimately lead to the destruction of a family.

Even though it is hard to find a large proportion of successful homeless who have uprooted themselves from the problem by empowering themselves to change their lives, I feel that education remains the key to understanding. I personally observe hundreds, even thousands of college level students who are challenged by even the basic intellectual tasks from understanding the importance of listening skills to ethics. Many students also come from broken homes with a tough uphill battle in this economy. It's easy for people to quit.

Our young people lack role models or as Chief would say, "self-heroes." I consistently do my part in finding the opportunity to build leaders in our community by pointing out the importance of completing education so that my students are strategic in making sound, ethical, and leadership choices which can place them in a better position in life so that they never end up like this. Times are very competitive even for the most basic of jobs.

Some homeless people are completely happy being homeless because they feel that they live life in its truest form of freedom, yet there remains great uncertainty for the homeless. The overall theme, which developed throughout my experience, is that happiness is living in the 'free zone' where a person can come and go as they please, care for others, and find inner peace. I respect that and I actually wish I had less worries than some of the people I met.

Unfortunately, since Venice Beach is not a public lecture hall for learning, looking at the homeless from a distance, people may misperceive and wrongly stereotype people like Pruitt as a pitiful homeless man, or just another person in life who couldn't live up to society's expectations of the man who captured the American Dream even though he believed whole-heartedly that he was defending that dream for all of us. I notice many people avoided him because he is missing an arm.

While knowledge is a beautiful thing, it can also bring disillusionment. Jane said, "I don't look at things anymore through the eyes of a tourist. Now I see things through the eyes of someone who knows the inner workings of this sub-culture." I also think that it is a major challenge going into the twenty first century to wake up the able from their habits and find justifiable, legitimate solutions to their social issues as the system finds ways for homeless and ex-offender population, many of which will be released back to our communities, to become more responsible to society and themselves. My fight is for the people who need help first, the mentally ill, the Vietnam, Korean, and Iraqi War Veterans, and the homeless who don't want to be homeless.

I also feel it is un-American to leave law abiding Veterans to fend for themselves, even for the Veterans who have mental illness. Suddenly, it doesn't matter that they are depressed and torn from trauma and mentally ill from the ravages of war, persecution, starvation? What message do we send our men and women in the Armed Forces? That what matters is being an able bodied soldier at the time the country needs bodies to fight for a cause only to be sacrificed for a government purpose. Our government spending is irresponsible and it is a disgrace that Veterans are out there begging for money and trying to find their next meal. I buy into the fact that not every individual has the strength to recover from what for many was a devastating war in Vietnam.

How dare some people have the nerve to treat law abiding Veterans in any way other than respectful. Don't forget what Tracy did to the veteran.

Many Veterans are in the high risk category for chronic homelessness. Didn't the government know that some Veterans had the potential for mental illness prior to sending them off to war or is there a cynical motivation behind sending people on the edge of mental illness that are sent as a way to rid them from society?

We also met a few true people who were visiting Venice this trip. Rob and Sheila are from Canada where the social problem of homelessness is not on as large a scale as the U.S. Rob, a defense attorney, said that you usually see people in the larger cities of Canada who are homeless like Edmonton, and the fact that the temperature plays a role at thirty below zero in the winter time, apparently keeps people motivated to find jobs and other means of survival in the country. According to CBC News, in 2007, Canada's homeless population is somewhere between 200,000 and 300,000 people, while another 1.7 million residents struggle with "housing affordability issues" (CBC News.ca, 2007). As I reported earlier in the book by comparison LA County has a roughly 250,000 homeless on any given night.

As I walked down the steps to the Venice Suites for the last time, I met Bonnie, a very sweet and intelligent woman from Texas. Bonnie is an artist by profession and she visits Venice Beach frequently because of its colorful characters and daughter Sabrina who lives here. Talking to Bonnie about the element here in Venice, we agreed that the faces have changed and so has the attitude towards people. Some have become disrespectful to the point that changes must be made. Bonnie asked me if my book has a conclusion, because she has been coming here for years and is still drawing hers. There will remain homeless people and we as a culture will continue to push the issue aside. When people in America who have power are deeply affected by this issue there will be change. The power is in the people to see to it that children especially, are no longer homeless.

Another way to address the homeless situation on Venice Beach is to ask people like the Chief who has credibility to sit at a roundtable discussion for his ideas on how to change things in a broken down system. The Chief has the answers. Chief has spent his life as a peaceful activist finding ways to improve humanity. He could actually help to improve the structure by mentoring others within this group. In a perfect world all people capable of working should fulfill their responsibility to society. Whether you agree or not, we do all have a sense of responsibility if we want to see changes. Putting all the blame on government solves nothing unless it affects the people in government whose communities have an abundance of homeless.

By creating temporary affordable housing using a "pilot" lottery system for those homeless willing and capable of winning a sense of responsibility back is another solution to the problem by having supportive housing services. This is an incentive. Call it the "Work

House" and reform the able homeless with the understanding that the program means business in terms of awakening a person and driving them to rebuild their lives.

Each facet of government should have the ability to come up with a list of "High Risk and Chronic" homeless so they can begin an intensive cost effective prevention strategy to keep the high risk out of the category along with finding a health care strategy which will enable the willing and wanting to work homeless like Joel. Joel would be an ideal person to mentor people who are on the brink of removing themselves from the homeless category. When the plan isn't working, constant reassessment should determine further steps to improve the program just like in the business world when a plan fails. Lets find a way to take a way from the social welfare system by identifying the less needy and supplementing and rewarding those who have been self motivated to find the right track to success. In the end everyone wins but the people who need motivation.

As for the helpless hopeless who could care less, many of these young drug addicted homeless people have other responsibilities, but they instead are so addicted, they ignore them. Some have children, don't pay child support and are perfectly capable of making an income to support their children, but they choose not to. If I didn't pay child support, I would be in jail. What makes them different? Thinking for the children here and on a greater scale, when children have no parents to look up to, it is a fact that many fall right into the pitfalls of a society. Some rejoice the opportunity to walk away from problems only to feed their drug and alcohol addictions while completely and irresponsibly ignoring their obligations. This only creates a bigger cycle of problems and children who grow into angry confused adults with no collaborative guidance from loving, caring parents who want their children to have what they never had. We only see the problems when it affects people who matter. Shouldn't everyone matter?

One homeless person who debated me about this issue said that we are literally stepping on his neck by polluting the air he breathes. Yet, he forgot that he breathes the same air and uses a toilet too in addition to supporting his needle habit. This generation has the world in their hands and if we just let the world be the way it is, hatred and bias towards others will never end.

Education is a beautiful thing. Some institutions are cookie cutter, but since I have the power to help create change in the way people think, I feel that my role of teaching people about this social issue will bring about that change and at the very least give a person a birds eye view of who the homeless are, and why some chose to live this way. I hope that our study of homelessness has been informative, thought-provoking, heart wrenching, but enlightening so that like me, you can find the courage in yourself to do something different that you have never done before with the goal to inspire others in mind. My glass heart breaks fast and gives in to the pain of others. Life is hard. I know.

As I do every summer, I gathered all of my clothes with the exception of what I would wear home and a few assorted items, and I leave them on our bench for the homeless. Last year I left at least 25 shirts, socks, shorts, water, and all of the left over food in my refrigerator. It is a small token of my unconditional love for people who stepped into my life for seconds in my lifetime, but whose faces and stories I will never forget. Every day though, I think of the suitcase that I have to pack when I leave this world. It comes down to whatever I leave behind as a memory. This book allows that opportunity regardless of what life has in store, to leave that memory of a journey to help people understand that homelessness, hunger, mental illness, and poverty is a worldwide problem.

In this world, people burn with pain and all they want is to fly with freedom, and some with sanity that they don't even know. As we know, with freedom comes a painful price. Life sometimes comes down to choices. I learned though that people sometimes have no choice, they give up when the world beats them, when they suffer from tragedy, adversity and addiction.

By choice, we went out of our way to meet, greet, and learn about the most unpopular segment of our society because it offered a perspective different from a textbook. I chose to live amongst the homeless and engage them so that I could help the public see life through their eyes, through their voices, and through their triumphs, tragedies, and memories.

We have much in common with homeless people. We are all human beings, we all make mistakes, and we all have problems. One person who I wished I had met is Coby McBee who was murdered savagely. That killer gets to breathe, live, and seek opportunity while Coby leaves behind a family who cares very much for him. I think his mother feels that he was taken for a reason. Let this book be a way to memorialize his life so that his children can somehow find reasons to forgive the person who took their father from them over a senseless disagreement which turned tragic.

For the sake of our children, I will put my footsteps in the sand and sacrifice time and money to ensure getting this message out. My determination is in making a difference for the betterment of humanity for future generations.

We want our children to change the world to be a better place, we want our leaders to be true leaders, and to use their power to defeat poverty, improve education, and create a medical system, which serves us all.

In this country instead of using taxpayers' money to fund wars and count body bags of American men and women who are shipped back with the American Flag on it, let's find a way to bring peace to our communities, nation, and world.

I am proud to be an American and to see that red white and blue flying proudly in the air. I believe in the people of this country and I know that as a nation we have it in us to bring about positive change. I have seen change in front of my eyes through the good deeds of my students who will do whatever it takes to volunteer time and help the less fortunate.

Another change in American culture is the treatment of the elderly, especially those who are homeless. In other cultures the elderly are revered.

I want my son to know it is sad to be homeless, but we can all help the homeless find a better way to live. Homeless children are innocent victims of the wrath of difficult situations. Unfortunately, they learn the hard way, early in life, the true sense of the word reality.

Life can change in a flash. There are so many beautiful things about Venice, the good natured and friendly people, and even many of the homeless.

At the end of the day and when all is said and done we reflect on this humbling experience, and conclude that the reality of the homeless in Venice Beach is that they spend 365 days out of the year trying to find peace, food, shelter, and happiness. While on the exterior there are many who help the homeless, also there are just as many who look the other way.

The key word is commitment by community, government, social service agencies, and the business community at large who have the ability to train and mold people into working-units who can be productive citizens, even if it is on a small scale through pilot programs. The United States delivers billions of dollars in foreign aid. In the land of the rich and famous, the perception for some cultures around the world is that the U.S. is also known as the stingiest.

Homelessness taught me countless valuable lessons, which I can now pass on to my students and my son. I hope it helps you, your students, you children, and the leaders of tomorrow to make a commitment to change the way we judge people. It opens a side to life that will help to change the overall public perception of the homeless and place a name with a face rather than a statistic and a number.

People within the community shunned us. Some perceived us as drug dealers and users, others looked down upon us, and some even thought we were undercover police officers. Again, it is amazing how perception plays such an integral role in our lives.

One of my missions is to be consistent in leaving my communication students with the message that we have to learn as much as we can from each other so that the world becomes a better place to live for the sake of our children.

Each of us has a destiny and path, but not all of us are born with parents who guide us, teachers who inspire us, and doctors who care for us, a nice hot meal from parents who nurture us. That is what makes social issues relevant to us all. Maybe its time to teach a new way, to reverse backward thinking when things don't work, and because our children are the one's coming up in the world, just maybe there will be less ignorance in the world so that we can solve this social problem which plaques our culture and cultures around the world so that people have a nice hot meal, and so that maybe the American Family will again thrive and move toward finding legitimate solutions to the problem. If we are not part of the solution then we are all part of the problem.

If there was a way to sweep the world's entire problem away it would be a miracle.

Ask yourself what difference can I make? Who am I? What is the legacy I wish to leave behind? What is my purpose here on this planet? Consider going to war against your own personal bias, dare to be different, see each homeless person we encounter and base the communication on individual experience. Let's find a way to root out homelessness in all of our communities so that this nation becomes the great nation it has the potential to be. First love, then peace will follow.

Bibliography

A status report on hunger and homelessness in America's Cities. Rep.No. The United States Conference of Mayors-Sodexho USA. Dec 2004 ed.

"All Homeless Kids - Even Couch-Surfers - Have Rights." <u>Daily Herald (Arlington Heights, IL)</u> 28 Jan. 2006: 19. 6 Sept. 2007.

"America's Homeless Children." <u>National Center of Family Homelessness</u>. 27 Oct. 2008 <http://www.familyhomelessness.org/pdf/fact_children.pdf>.

Antunes, Antonio, Ana Machado, Joao Crespo, and Samuel Silva. <u>Black Power</u>. 29 Oct. 2008 <http://www.esec-nuno-alvares.rcts.pt/professores/ingles/apontamentos/blackpower.pdf>.

Baumohl, Jim, ed. <u>Homelessness in America</u>. Phoenix: Oryx Press, 1996. 6 Sept. 2007

Baum, Alice S., and Donald W. Burnes. <u>A Nation in Denial: The Truth about Homelessness</u>. Boulder, CO: Westview P, 1993. 1-247.

"Columbia Encyclopedia: anti–Vietnam War movement." <u>Anti–Vietnam War movement</u>. Answers.com. 29 Oct. 2008 <opposition to the war grew as television and press coverage graphically showed the suffering of both civilians and conscripts>.

"Comprehensive Strategy to End Homelessness Released to Public." http://www.bringlahome.org/. 4 Apr. 2006. The Economic Roundtable. 20 Aug. 2006 <http://lacounty.info/bos/sop/supdocs/24276.pdf>.

"Counterculture." Wikipedia.Com. 11 Oct. 2007 <http://en.wikipedia.org/wiki/Counterculture>.

Duffy, Maureen P., and Scott Edward Gillig, eds. Teen Gangs: A Global View. Westport, CT: Greenwood Press, 2004. 6 Sept. 2007

"Epidemic of Hate Crimes Against Homeless People." Street Spirit Mar. 2005, March 2006 ed.

Evry, Marta. "Man fatally stabbed near Boardwalk Thurs., July 20th." Venice Forum 27 July 2006. http://www.veniceforum.org. 20 Aug. 2006 <http://www.argonautnewspaper.com/articles/2006/07/27/news_-_features/venice/b1v.txt>.

"Murder of Venice homeless goes unnoticed." Venice Forum 16 Feb. 2006. http://www.veniceforum.org. 20 Aug. 2006. 20 Aug. 2006 <http://www.veniceforum.org/?q=taxonomy/page/or/8>.

Evaluation of Multi-Jurisdictional. Http://www.oes.ca.gov/WebPage/oeswebsite.nsf/PDF/Evaluation%20of%20Multi-Jurisdictional%20Drug%20Task%20Forces%20in%20California/$file/MJTFrpt.pdf. Vers. July 2003. July 2003. The California State University,. 25 Oct. 2008 <http://www.oes.ca.gov/webpage/oeswebsite.nsf/pdf/evaluation%20of%20multi-

jurisdictional%20drug%20task%20forces%20in%20california/$file/mj
tfrpt.pdf>.

Fabian Gonzalez. "Ronald Reagan: The Bad and the Ugly."
Editorial. <u>Daily Nugget San Francisco</u> 08 June 2004.

"Facts and Figures." <u>More than 100,000 Homeless Children</u>. June
2008. Horizons for Homeless Children. 27 Oct. 2008
<http://www.horizonsforhomelesschildren.org/>.

"Facts and Myths about Mental Illness." <u>Mental Health America
of</u>. 28 Oct. 2008. Mental Health America of. 29 Oct. 2008
<http://www.mhagstl.org/myths.htm>.

Fatout, Marian F. <u>Children in Groups: A Social Work Perspective</u>.
Westport, CT: Auburn House, 1996. 6 Sept. 2007

"FILM-MAKER HITS OUT AT PLIGHT OF HOMELESS; Cathy
Come Home Writer at Charity Event." <u>Coventry Evening Telegraph
(England)</u> 8 June 2007: 1. Sept. 2007.

"Food Insecurity and Hunger in Los Angeles." <u>HandsNet Human
Services News</u> (2006). 09 June 2006
<http://webclipper.handsnet.org/mt-
static/archives/2006/06/food_insecurity.html>.

"Fury over Plan for Homeless Shelter; CAMPAIGN: Anonymous
Leaflet Stirs Up Opposition among Building's Neighbours." <u>Coventry
Evening Telegraph (England)</u> 6 Mar. 2007: 9. 6 Sept. 2007

"HIV/AIDS Cases By County in California." <u>Office of AIDS -
2008 Monthly HIV/AIDS Statistics</u>. 30 Sept. 2008. California
Department of Public Health. 27 Oct. 2008

<http://ww2.cdph.ca.gov/data/statistics/documents/oa-2008-09-aidsmerged.pdf>.

"Homeless Get Helping Hand Back into Work; THRIVE THROUGH CORPORATE SOCIAL RESPONSIBILITY." The Birmingham Post (England) 9 May 2006: 25. 6 Sept. 2007

"Helping Homeless Vets." The Register-Guard (Eugene, OR) 15 Nov. 2006: A8. 6 Sept. 2007

"Homelessness 'chronic' in Canada: study." 26 June 2007. 30 Oct. 2008 <http://www.cbc.ca/canada/story/2007/06/26/shelter.html>.

"Homeless Housing Strategy Launched." The Birmingham Post (England) 7 Dec. 2005: 4. 6 Sept. 2007

"Homeless in America." Homeless in America. 19 Apr. 2004. Washington Profile. 27 Oct. 2008 <http://www.washprofile.org/en/node/2295>.

"Homelessness & Poverty." Anitraweb.Org. 29 Nov. 2002. 21 Oct. 2007 <http://anitraweb.org/homelessness/faqs/terminology.html>;.

"Homelessness-What's the Real Solution?" Youth Noise.Com. 02 June 2007 <http://www.youthnoise.com/page.php?page_id=2247>;.

Hill, Nathan. "Our Beleaguered Beaches." E MAGAZINE.COM May 1999: 16.

"Homeless Education." New York Times [Greensboro, NC] Mar. 2006, National Center for Homeless Education ed.: 3.

"Homelessness." Hastings Borough Council. 02 Dec. 2005. 08 Aug. 2007 <http://www.hastings.gov.uk/housing_advice/homelessness.aspx>;.

"Homeless Facts." <u>Goodwill Inn</u> . 20 Aug. 2006. Goodwill Industries of Northern Michigan, Inc. 20 Aug. 2006 <http://www.goodwillinn.org/facts.htm>.

"Homelessness: Reviewing the Facts." <u>Mental Health America</u>. National Mental Health Association. 27 Oct. 2008 <http://www1.nmha.org/homeless/homelessnessfacts.cfm>.

"Hunger, Homelessness On the Rise in Major U.S. Cities." <u>U.S. Mayor Newspaper</u> 14 Jan. 2008.

"http://en.wikipedia.org/wiki/ Arnold_Schwarzenegger#Personal_background." <u>http://en.wikipedia.org</u>. Wikimedia Foundation. 20 Aug. 2006 <http://http://en.wikipedia.org>.

<u>http://www.ferraricarrental.com</u>. 20 Aug. 2006 <http://www. ferraricarrental.com/places/Venice-Beach-California.htm>.

"http://www.trulia.com/city/CA/Beverly_Hills/." <u>Trulia Real Estate of Los Angeles</u>. 20 Aug. 2006. 20 Aug. 2006 <http://www.trulia.com/CA/Los_Angeles/>.

<u>http://www.weingart.org/institute/</u>. Institute for the Study of Homelessness and Poverty. 20 Aug. 2006 <http://www.weingart.org/ institute/research/facts/pdf/JustTheFactsHomelessnessLA.pdf>.

HUD. Los Angeles Homeless Services Authority. <u>2004 Los Angeles Continuum Care Awards</u>. Los Angeles: Los Angeles Homeless Services Authority. <u>www.lahsa.org</u>. 2004. A Joint Powers Authority Created by the City and County of Los Angeles. 23 Aug. 2006 <http://www.lahsa.org/pdfs/Current/2004%20CoC%20Awards.pdf>.

Karlinsky, Neal. "Worldwide News with Charles Gibson." Worldwide News with Charles Gibson. ABC NEWS. 24 Nov. 2008.

Kasindorf, Martin. "Nation Taking a New Look At Homelessness, Solutions." USA Today. 11 Oct. 2005. 06 June 2007 <http://www.usatoday.com/news/nation/2005-10-11-homeless-cover_x.htm?csp=34>;.

Kusmer, Kenneth L. Down and Out, on the Road: The Homeless in American History. New York: Oxford University Press, 2003. 6 Sept. 2007

LAPD COMPSTAT Citywide Crime Statistics July 29, 2006. Raw data. 29 July 2006.

"Los Angeles Regional Food Bank." Los Angeles Regional Food Bank. Los Angeles Regional Food Bank. <http://www.lafoodbank.org/>.

LAPD FOIA Crime Data. Raw data. 2006.

"LAPD Arrest Homeless At Venice Beach." You Tube.Com. 07 Jan. 2007. 06 June 2007 <http://www.youtube.com/watch?v=1z9PMDCZt6Y>.

"Matrix: Homelessness Services." Substance Abuse and Mental Health Services Administration. 29 June 2006. 11 July 2007 <http://www.samhsa.gov/Matrix/statistics_homeless.aspx>.

Miniter, Richard. "Crime Wave May Turn L.A. Tide." Insight on the News 14 June 1993: 6+. 6 Sept. 2007

"MORBID CURIOSITY: Celebrity Tombstones Across America." www.morbid-curiosity.com. 24 Aug. 2004. Morbid Curiosity Website

Designed and Operated by: Elaine McCarthy. 20 Aug. 2006 <http://www.morbid-curiosity.com/id153.htm>.

Myers, Dowell, Baer, William C, Choi,, and Seong-Youn. "The changing Problem of Overcrowded Housing." Journal of the American Planning Association 62 (Winter 96): 66-84. http://www-rcf.usc.edu/~dowell/pdf/changi.pdf

"Myths & Facts." coe.west.asu.edu. Homeless Education & Ne-glected/Delinquent Programs. 20 Aug. 2006 <http://coe.west.asu.edu/homeless/myths.htm>.

National Coalition for the Homeless. Hate Crimes Against People Experiencing Homelessness. June 2006. 1 of 6. http://www.nationalhomeless.org. 20 Aug. 2006 <http://www.nationalhomeless.org/publications/facts/Hatecrimes.pdf>.

Neiman, David. "Venice Beach California." Travel Channel News. www.Travel.Discovery.com. 20 Aug. 2006. 20 Aug. 2006 <http://travel.discovery.com/convergence/beachweek/guide/beaches/venicebeach.html>.

Neuman, Elena. "Cities Get Tough with the Homeless." Insight on the News 14 Feb. 1994: 6+.

"1 Windward Circle Neighborhood Profile Abbot Kinney Venice-of-America ." Los Angeles Conservancy. 20 Aug. 2006 <http://www.laconservancy.org/initiatives/windward.pdf>.

Rieckhoff, Paul. "O'Reilly Downplays Number of Homeless Veterans." Guerilla News Network. 17 Jan. 2008.Guerilla News Network.30 Oct. 2008

<http://www.gnn.tv/articles/3496/o_reilly_downplays_number_of_ho meless_veterans>.

Paulsen, Monte. "Seven Solutions to Homelessness." The Tyee 08 Jan. 2007. 10 Aug. 2007

<http://thetyee.ca/Views/2007/01/08/HomelessSolutions/>;.

"Peyote." Peyote. 27 Oct. 2008

<http://www.dkosopedia.com/wiki/peyote>.

"Preventing Homelessness in America." Solutions for America. Thriving Neighborhoods Solutions for America University of Richmond. 20 Oct. 2007

<http://www.solutionsforamerica.org/thrivingneigh/homelessness. html>.

"Rise in Hate Crimes." Street Spirit (2005). http://www.createpeaceathome.org/streetspirit/2005/september2005/ris einhatecrimes.htm. 20 Oct. 2007.

Public Policy and Hate-Motivated Crimes Against Homeless Individuals. Http://www.nationalhomeless.org/civilrights/JointPositionStatement.p df. Aug. 2008. <http://www.nationalhomeless.org/civilrights/jointpositionstatement.pdf>.

"Strides Help Homeless to Step in Right Direction." The Washington Times 17 Nov. 2006: B02. 6 Sept. 2007

"Take Action Against NYC's Toughest Problems." United Way of New York City. 09 Aug. 2007 <http://www.unitedwaynyc.org/>;.

"The Sit in Movement." <u>ENotes</u>. 08 June 2007 <http://www.enotes.com/1960-lifestyles-social-trends-american-decades/sit-movement>.

Stanton, Jeffrey. "Windward Circle Neighborhood Profile." Los Angeles Conservancy. 31 Oct. 2008 <http://www.laconservancy.org/initiatives/windward.pdf>.

"THRIVE THROUGH CORPORATE SOCIAL RESPONSIBILITY: Helping Homeless Get Back to Work." <u>The Birmingham Post (England)</u> 25 Apr. 2006: 25. 6 Sept. 2007

Tugend, Alina. "The Least Affordable Place to Live? Try Salinas." <u>New York Times</u> [New York] 7 May 2006, natl ed., sec. Real Estate <u>The New York Times</u>. New York Times.com. 20 Aug. 2006 <http://newyorktimes.com>.

Vegre, Arthur C. "George Freeth: King of the Surfers and California's Forgotten Hero." <u>California History</u> Summer 2001: 83+.

"UNITED STATES Homeless Statistics." <u>UNITED STATES Homeless Statistics</u>. Freedom Tracks Music Records. 30 Oct. 2008 <http://www.freedomtracks.com/statistics.html>.

<u>U.S. Department of Labor Center for Faith Based & Community Initiatives</u>. USA. U.S. Department of Labor. Center for Faith-Based & Community Initiatives. 30 Oct. 2008. U.S. Department of Labor. 30 Oct. 2008 <http://www.dol.gov/cfbci/reentry.htm>.

<u>Venice California History Website</u>. 6 June 2005. The material is copyrighted © 1996 to 2005 by Jeffrey Stanton. . 20 Aug. 2006 <http://naid.ucla.edu/venice/>.

Washington Profile. http://www.washprofile.org. 18 Aug. 2006. World Security Institute.

White House Faith Based and Community Initiatives'. USA. The White House George W. Bush. President of the United States. Office of the President of The United States. 30 Oct. 2008 <http://www.whitehouse.gov/government/fbci/pri.html>.

Whyte, Alan. "Nearly half of New York City's homeless are children." Nearly half of New York City's homeless are children. 07 Jan. 2004. Published by the International Committee of the Fourth International (ICFI). 27 Oct. 2008 <http://www.wsws.org/articles/2004/jan2004/nyc-j07.shtml>.

Wyman, June R. "Drug Abuse Among Runaway and Homeless Youths Calls for Focused Outreach Solutions." May-June 1997. National Institutes of Health. 29 Oct. 2008 <http://www.nida.nih.gov /nida_notes/nnvol12n3/runaway.html>.

William G. O'Connell, M.A.

Bill O'Connell is a former professional model and reporter for The McGraw-Hill Companies. He is currently a tenured Assistant Professor of Communication at Suffolk County Community College's Grant Campus in Brentwood, New York.

A 1981, graduate of Leto Comprehensive High School in Tampa, Florida, he received his BA in American Studies/Journalism from the State University of New York, College at Old Westbury, and an MA in Communication Arts from New York Institute of Technology.

Bill's community service track record is extensive: This year he participated in the "Toys for Cancer Kids" toy drive for the holiday season for children with cancer. He has raised tens of thousands of dollars to *Feed the Hungry* in the *Long Island Cares* campaign as well as the *Thanksgiving Day Turkey Drive* which feeds more than 100 local families each year at the college. Bill has also been involved in countless Blood Drives, and with the help of the local community in East Islip held one of the largest drives in the state on *"The Night for Colin"* Bone Marrow Blood Drive in 2000 to save his son Colin from AML Leukemia. CBS News, WB-11, CBS Radio, WBAB Radio, LI News, and News 55 all covered the event. His endless contributions to the community are unwavering. He began the *"Dollar for Colin Drive"* to raise money for childhood cancer research this year with the help of students and the SCCC Honors program. This drive will enable dying children to have a fighting chance. In the classroom his small group communication class held a very successful clothing drive for Long Island's PRONTO homeless shelter in Brentwood, NY to clothe the homeless. The group collected more than 20 bags of clothes.

Bill has won many awards in education.

- 2004, Certificate of Achievement from Suffolk County Executive Steve Levy, for Co-Advisor to New York State Champion Speech and Debate team at SCCC
- 2004, Certificate of Excellence for Outstanding Advisor at SCCC, for Co-Advisor to New York State Champion Speech and Debate team at SCCC

- 2004, Presidential Citation from College President Dr. Shirley Robinson Pippins for Co-Advisor to New York State Champion Speech and Debate Team
- 1987, as President of the Human Resources Club he was awarded Outstanding Service Award to the Students at Suffolk Community College's Western Campus
- In 1989, he received all-academic honors for outstanding achievement at SUNY College Old Westbury, where he was also selected for a TV internship at WCBS-TV, Channel Two News with Health and Science Reporter, Earl Ubell.

In addition to teaching, Bill played a role in the College Success Program, was Advisor to the Western Student Press at the Grant Campus, and he was co-coach and advisor for the New York State Championship Speech and Debate team in 2004 for SCCC at Grant Campus. The team is the only junior college in the 58-year history of speech and debate to win a state title against four-year universities. Besides teaching at Suffolk full-time, he has taught at St. Joseph's College, Five Towns College, and Nassau Community College.